VICTIMS OF
TEEN VIOLENCE

VICTIMS OF TEEN VIOLENCE

DISCARD

Karen Zeinert

—Issues in Focus—

ENSLOW PUBLISHERS, INC.

44 Fadem Road	P.O. Box 38
Box 699	Aldershot
Springfield, N.J. 07081	Hants GU12 6BP
U.S.A.	U.K.

362.88
Z46v

Copyright © 1996 by Karen Zeinert

All rights reserved.

No part of this book may be reproduced by any means without the written permission of the publisher.

Library of Congress Cataloging-in-Publication Data

Zeinert, Karen.
    Victims of teen violence / Karen Zeinert.
        p. cm. — (Issues in focus)
    Includes bibliographical references and index.
    Summary: Relates accounts of teen violence in school, at home, among friends, and in public places, and offers information for victims about what to do and where to get help.
    ISBN 0-89490-737-9
    1. Victims of crimes—United States—Juvenile literature. 2. Juvenile delinquency—United States—Juvenile literature. 3. Violent crimes—United States—Juvenile literature. [1. Victims of crimes. 2. Juvenile delinquency. 3. Violent crimes. 4. Violence. 5. Crime.] I. Title. II. Series: Issues in focus (Hillside, N.J.)
    HV6250.3.U5Z45 1996
    362.88—dc20   95-42133
                                          CIP
                                          AC

Printed in the United States of America

10 9 8 7 6 5 4 3 2 1

Illustration Credits: Courtesy of Candy Lightner, p. 99; Dan Reiland/ *Eau Claire Leader-Telegram*, pp. 60, 84; Frank Anderson/*Lexington Herald-Leader*, p. 9; Photograph by James Gill, reproduced by permission from Wisconsin Public Television, p. 40; John Flavell/*The Daily Independent*, pp. 17, 22, 31, 88, 106; John A. Zeinert, pp. 46, 68, 72, 91; *Oshkosh Northwestern*, p. 51; Richard Ballin/Appleton Medical Center, p. 82; Ronald M. Overdahl/*Milwaukee Journal*, p. 65; Wisconsin Department of Justice (photo, John A. Zeinert), pp. 101, 103.

Cover Illustration: John A. Zeinert.

Contents

1

Teen Violence

On January 18, 1993, high school English teacher Deanna McDavid was correcting papers and her students were working at their desks when Scott Pennington, an unpopular honor student, entered the Grayson, Kentucky, classroom. No one noticed Scott as he walked toward his teacher's desk, until he fired a revolver he had kept concealed in his jacket. Scott's shot, which just missed Mrs. McDavid, astonished her and her students, who at first thought the startling scene before them was some kind of prank. But when Scott fired again, everyone quickly realized this was not a joke. Scott's second shot hit and killed McDavid, and as she slumped to the floor, stunned students stared in horror at her lifeless body.

The sound of gunfire also alarmed people outside the

classroom, and several, including Marvin Hicks, the school's custodian, raced toward McDavid's room. Hicks was the first to reach the door. As he entered the room, Scott turned and aimed at the janitor. While classmates held their breath, Scott pulled the trigger for the third time that day, killing Hicks.

Pennington then shifted his attention to his dazed and distraught classmates. After telling them that he had a bullet for each of them, he sneered and taunted them, wondering aloud if they liked him now. Fearing for their lives, the students were too terrified to say or do anything, believing that any reaction would be deadly. As Scott baited his hostages, one girl began a farewell note to her parents, certain that she would never see them again.

After what seemed to the students like an eternity, Pennington's mood changed. He decided to allow some—then all—of his hostages to leave the room one or two at a time. When police officers arrived, Scott surrendered peacefully.

The murders committed that day shocked the community, a small town that, until then, had experienced little violent crime. Unfortunately though, the killings were not all that unusual, for violence is commonplace in the United States, even when it is committed by teenagers.

Violent Crime in America

Violent crimes are criminal acts that pose the greatest threat to physical safety. These crimes include: murder (deliberately taking someone's life); rape (using force or threat of force to sexually violate someone, usually a female); robbery (taking an item of value from a person

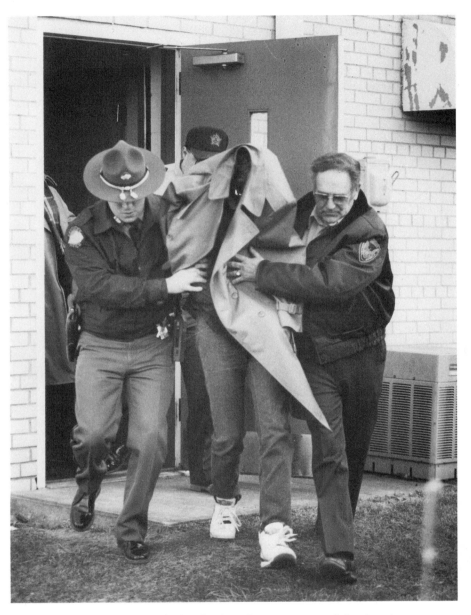

Scott Pennington, a high school student, was arrested for shooting his English teacher, Deanna McDavid, and the school's custodian, Marvin Hicks.

by use of force or threat of force); assault (attacking a person to inflict bodily harm); and arson (maliciously burning a home or building).

It is difficult to determine how many violent crimes take place in the United States each year, for records from various sources differ greatly. For example, police files indicate that out of every hundred thousand people in the United States seven hundred fifty are victims of violent crimes. This means that one American is victimized every sixteen seconds. However, police files contain information only about events that have been reported, and some experts on crime believe that as many as half of the violent acts committed in the United States are not reported to law officials. Others believe that the number of unreported crimes is even higher.

Looking for Victims

To try to get a better idea of the actual number of criminal acts—violent and nonviolent—the U.S. Department of Justice conducts annual studies to find all victims. These studies involve many people: during one twenty-year project, for example, interviewers talked to more than 800 million Americans.

Once the interviewers have finished gathering their information, statistical experts analyze the data, a difficult and time-consuming task. These experts try to determine how many people throughout the country have been victimized by developing formulas based on the number of people who said they were assaulted, robbed, or raped. If ten out of every thousand people interviewed were assaulted, the experts must decide whether this average would be true for all people in the United States. To do this, they must determine whether the victims interviewed truly represent all Americans. Did they represent all sections of the United States? All races? All ages?

Statistical experts also look for trends. Are certain crimes on the rise? Are particular groups of people—men, women, African Americans, or Latinos, for example—more likely to become victims than are other groups?

Results of Studies

The results of the department's studies, especially the twenty-year project, were surprising and shocking. One of the worst years crimewise was 1981. Since then, the total number of criminal acts has gone down significantly because the number of nonviolent crimes has decreased. The fact that the total number of crimes is declining, however, would surprise most Americans; in recent polls, almost 90 percent of people polled believe that the crime rate is rising—rapidly.

The belief that crime is increasing is the result of the extensive publicity that violent attacks receive. Here there is little to cheer about. More than 10 million violent crimes were committed in 1993, the last year for which statistics were available. This was an increase of more than six hundred thousand criminal acts over the previous year. In short, violent acts account for a much larger percentage of the total number of crimes than ever before.

The increase in violent crime is due in large part to a

WHO ARE THE VICTIMS OF VIOLENT CRIMES?

Some Americans are more at risk of becoming victims of violent crime than are others. The chart below compares two races that make up the vast majority of victims of all violent crimes in the United States. The number given for each entry is the average number of people victimized each year for every 1,000 people in a particular group. For example, out of every 1,000 black male teens, 113 are victimized each year.

113 — Teenage black males

94 — Teenage black females
90 — Teenage white males

80 — Young adult black males

57 — Young adult black females
55 — Teenage white females
52 — Young adult white males

38 — Young adult white females
35 — Adult black males

18 — Adult white males
15 — Adult white females
13 — Adult black females
12 — Elderly black males
10 — Elderly black females
6 — Elderly white males
3 — Elderly white females[1]

Note: young adults, 20–34; adults, 35–64; elderly, 65 and over.

dramatic rise in the number of violent acts committed by teenagers. Two different sources show how serious this problem is at present. In 1994, the Federal Bureau of Investigation (FBI) announced that, according to its records, the number of young people under the age of eighteen who had been arrested for murder that year was nearly double the number of teens arrested for the same crime in 1985. However, the number of teens in the United States was almost the same in 1994 as it was in 1985. In comparison, the number of adults arrested for murder in 1994 was 5 percent greater than the number arrested in 1985 even though the adult population was 10 percent larger than it had been in 1985. Also, murder is not the only crime skyrocketing among teens. The Office of Juvenile Justice and Delinquency Prevention reported that the rate of arrests for all violent crimes committed by teenagers has increased by 67 percent since 1985.

Even more shocking is the outlook for the future if the current trend of more teens committing violent acts continues. The number of teens in America will increase by 23 percent by the year 2005 due to a population surge in the late 1980s and early 1990s. As a result, experts on juvenile crime and researchers such as James Fox of Northeastern University in Boston have predicted not just an increase in violence, but "an epidemic of teenage crime."[2]

Teenage Criminals

Who are the violent teens? Records of juveniles recently held in custody indicate that 42 percent were African Americans, 40 percent were whites, and more than 15

WHO ARE THE VIOLENT OFFENDERS?

More than 70 percent of all violent crimes are committed by a lone assailant who is:

- Between ages fifteen and seventeen in 11 percent of the victimizations.

- Between ages eighteen and twenty in 15 percent of the victimizations.

- Between ages twenty-one and twenty-nine in 33 percent of the victimizations.

- Age thirty or over in 33 percent of the victimizations.

- Male in 85 percent of the victimizations.

- White in 64 percent of the victimizations.

- Black in 28 percent of the victimizations.

- Under the influence of drugs or alcohol in 54 percent of the victimizations.[3]

percent were Latinos; the rest, a little over 2 percent, were from a variety of minority groups. Records also indicate that 88 percent of the teens in custody were males.[4]

The current breakdown of teens being arrested today reflects a change in who is becoming a violent juvenile. More girls, African Americans, and other minorities are being arrested than ever before—at a younger age.

Causes of Teenage Violence

The teenage years are unique. Teens have unlimited energy and an unending need for action. Many are also somewhat attracted to violence: horror films and scary novels are especially popular with this group. The teenage years are also the time when young people seek independence, and to gain this independence they often challenge authority. Because they are so full of life, teens sometimes feel invincible. On the other hand, many a teen's self-esteem is not so invincible. Insults—real or imagined—can cause great anger and anguish at any age, but they are especially painful to teens trying to find acceptance among their peers. This mix of emotions and needs puts teenagers in a vulnerable position, and when other factors are present, some teens commit violent acts.

Experts on juveniles have argued for years about why some children become criminals. These experts include social workers, psychologists, school counselors, counselors in detention centers, judges, lawyers, and even physicians who work in emergency rooms and routinely deal with the results of teen violence. Although not all of these experts agree on the primary cause, most list at

15

least five things they believe contribute to teen violence: abusive parents; the prevalence of violence in the media; the availability of weapons, especially guns; poverty; and drugs.

Children living in homes where parents are abusive receive little love and lack positive role models. As a result, these children do not learn how to build satisfying relationships. These children also have few opportunities to build self-esteem. Furthermore, when they receive or witness verbal and physical abuse on a regular basis, violence becomes an acceptable reaction, and they, in turn, lash out whenever they feel the need to do so.

Juvenile crime experts also cite the prevalence of violence in the media as a factor in teen violence. They are especially critical of films such as *Total Recall*, in which several people explode when they are tossed out into the vacuum that surrounds Mars, the story's setting. The worst of the villains in this film, however, does not die so simple a death. Instead, during a fight with the hero on a platform surrounded by machinery, the villain's arms are severed. As he—or what remains of him—falls from the platform, the hero is shown holding two bloody stumps. In another smash hit *Die Hard 2*, the sequel to *Die Hard*, the hero stabs a man in the brain by pushing an icicle through the victim's eye socket. This hit was so successful, its filmmaker decided to make a third movie with the same hero and action format, *Die Hard with a Vengeance*. Other filmmakers, including the makers of *Batman Forever*, were impressed by the success of the *Die Hard* series and the number of violent films increased rather than decreased, despite the critics' uproar.

One of the most outspoken critics of violence in the

Scott Pennington did not get along well with his peers. This lonely, angry teenager, shown here in court, was sentenced to life for his crimes. He will not be eligible for parole for twenty-five years.

media is Dr. Deborah Prothrow-Stith. Prothrow-Stith spent most of her medical internship in the emergency room of a Boston hospital. Appalled by the number of wounded and dying teens brought to the hospital as the result of teen violence, Prothrow-Stith began to look for the causes of these crimes, hoping to find some way to stop the violence. After years of study, she concluded that films that glamorize violence contribute to teen violence, because such films tell children that violence is an acceptable way of solving problems. "Any amount of killing is all right, so long as one's cause is just," she said, referring to the messages in violent films. "Violence is a hero's way to solve problems."[5]

Dr. Prothrow-Stith is not the only professional to hold this opinion. Many psychologists insist that violence in the media has a negative effect on children. They point to the growing body of research that tends to support the argument that the more violence children watch on television, the more aggressive they become. However, media executives repeatedly have denied any link between violent films and aggression.

Another cause of teen violence on the experts' list is the availability of guns. There are currently more than 50 million handguns in circulation in the United States. Children brag about how easy it is to buy guns or, if funds are short, how easy it is to rent weapons by the hour from acquaintances. Because guns are available, children who used to solve their differences by arguing or even fist fighting, now settle their differences with weapons. One young man in Detroit said, "There are no more fights in Detroit. It's just guns now."[6] Not every child packing a gun will become a murderer, but the availability of such weapons makes it easy for an angry or impulsive youth to kill or maim someone without much thought, skill, or courage.

Experts on crime also believe that poverty causes teen violence. American society places a lot of emphasis on material things and feeling good. Advertisements routinely push certain clothes or particular brands of shoes, and the desire to own these products, which seem to provide instant happiness and success in the ads, is strong among teens, especially those who are unhappy or lack self-esteem. According to psychologist Alvin Poussaint, "The guy on the block who has the new Nike sneaker[s] or jacket is considered a big shot."[7]

Because these things are so important, poor teens who believe violence is acceptable may assault others so that they can obtain a coveted item. C. C. Lavant, who grew up in a poverty-stricken area, said, "A lot of kids are obsessed with material things. . . . If they don't have the Adidas and Air Jordan sneakers, the Dior sweat suits, they feel ashamed. That's when they turn to violence."[8]

In addition, many poor teens feel they have little chance of legally escaping poverty. They cannot afford to go to college, nor can they find good jobs. As a result, they may turn to violence to get money or assault others just out of anger and frustration.

A fifth cause of teen violence cited by experts is the demand for illegal drugs in our society. While some violent teens steal so that they can support a drug habit, most sell drugs to make money, especially in poverty-stricken areas. Because drug trafficking is so lucrative, dealers fight among themselves over who will sell crack cocaine or other addictive products in a particular area, and many deaths have been attributed to these fights.

Even though there is some agreement among experts as to what causes teen violence, there is little agreement about what should be done to stop the violence. Should officials remove children from their homes more quickly when abuse is suspected? Limit the amount of violence in the media? Outlaw guns? Develop new antipoverty programs? Clearly, there are no simple answers. Meanwhile, as the arguments continue, the number of victims of teen violence—most of them children—continues to grow in our schools, homes, and public places.

Past and Future Victims of Teen Violence

Learning more about the victims of teen violence will not make the violence go away, but it will help determine what kind of help victims need. In addition, studying their stories will help us to better understand who is at risk, making it possible to alert and protect would-be victims in the future—a group that could very well include you and me.

2

Victims in Schools

Unfortunately, the murders in Mrs. McDavid's Kentucky classroom were not the only violent incidents to occur in America's schools. The targets, however, are usually the assailants' classmates, not teachers and custodians. In California and New York, for instance, teens have been shot to death in school hallways. In Massachusetts, a teenager was beaten to death by a fifteen-year-old wielding a baseball bat; another was killed in his social studies class by three students armed with clubs and knives. In Florida, a high school senior was shot dead by another boy in a fight over a girl.

Attempted murders have also made the headlines. An angry student fired at his classmates in Texas after a pep rally, leaving six wounded. In Wisconsin, a gun-toting teen was let into a high school that kept its doors locked

Marvin Hicks, a school custodian, was shot dead in school by Scott Pennington. Hicks was popular with both students and teachers.

by a friend who was inside the building. The friend also led the assailant to the intended victim, with whom the assailant had quarreled previously. The armed teen then fired several shots, attempting to kill the boy. In Orlando, Florida, a fifteen-year-old girl attacked another girl, repeatedly slashing her with a knife. In fact, the fear of dying in a school building has become so real that, as one principal reported, "When one kid tells another one . . . 'I'm gonna kill you,' [he or she takes] it seriously."[1]

Perhaps as alarming as the attacks is the attitude shown not only by the assailants, but by some other students as well. When a group of high school students was interviewed, 20 percent said that it was all right to shoot someone "who has stolen something from you." About half of the students who thought that it was all right to shoot a thief also thought it was all right to shoot someone "who had done something to offend or insult you."[2]

The attitude that violence is acceptable is not limited to particular schools. The commonly held belief among the public is that only students in poverty-stricken areas in large cities are at risk, but this is not true. In 1993, researchers at Xavier University in Ohio questioned principals about violent incidents in their schools to try to determine where violent incidents were happening. More than one thousand school districts across the nation participated in the study. Principals reported violent incidents throughout the country; 64 percent of the principals in urban areas, 54 percent in suburban districts, and 46 percent in rural areas reported a dramatic increase in violent events in their schools between 1988 and 1993.[3]

Witness Victims

Although the victims of murderous attacks and their families suffer the greatest losses, they are not the only victims of these crimes. Witnesses also suffer. The brutal scenes they see not only cause great anguish but also destroy their sense of safety. As a result, most become so fearful that their daily routines are severely altered.

The reactions of the students to the shootings in Deanna McDavid's classroom are typical. Some of these teens were afraid to go to sleep at night unless a parent was in the room to protect them. One girl was so traumatized she refused to enter the school building again, and she had to finish her education at home. Another student asked to be allowed to sit next to the door in all of his classes from then on, so that he might escape more easily if another hostage situation occurred. Counseling sessions were held at the school, but according to one counselor there, "For the students who were in the room or outside in the hall, the memory of the shootings will never go away."[4]

Murder and attempted murder in school receive a lot of attention because these acts are so shocking; after all, schools are supposed to be safe places. But murder is hardly the only crime frightening students today; they are also afraid of becoming the targets of vicious assaults and robberies.

Teen Assaults in Schools

There are about 21 million teenage students in the United States today. Approximately 89 percent of them attend public schools; the rest are taught in private institutions or tutored at home. The latest statistics from the Justice Department show that more than 2 million violent crimes are committed in and around schools by

STUDENT WORRIES ABOUT SAFETY IN SCHOOL

Recently, twenty-five hundred students who expressed fear about their safety in school were asked to identify what worried them. The chart below contains their greatest concerns. Note the difference among grade levels.

FEAR	ELEMENTARY	JUNIOR HIGH	SENIOR HIGH
Weapons	11 percent	19 percent	20 percent
Gangs	7 percent	10 percent	13 percent
Fights	10 percent	20 percent	15 percent
Physical Abuse/ Bullies	12 percent	9 percent	4 percent[5]

teens each year. This means that approximately ten thousand teenagers are attacked by their peers every day that school is in session. This averages out to about sixteen hundred assaults every hour.

Students who have been victimized by teens report a variety of attacks: all-out fighting, pushing, slapping, and kicking. Others have been threatened with guns, knives, or other dangerous objects.

The type of assault varies from grade to grade. In general, attacks by teens are more serious among older students; assaults involving a knife or gun are six times more likely to occur among students in grades ten through twelve than they are in grades six through nine.

The number of victims involved in serious fights also varies from grade to grade. For example, 14 percent of sixth-graders reported being involved in a fight, compared to 22 percent of tenth-graders.[6] However, there is a steady drop in fighting between grades ten and twelve.[7]

Besides age, there are a number of other factors that make some students more vulnerable to attack than others. Public school students are more likely to be victimized than teens who attend private institutions. Students who go to schools where drugs are available are also more at risk. In addition, children who are perceived to be different from most of their peers—minorities, homosexuals, and recent immigrants, for example—are more likely to be attacked than others, especially in middle schools.[8]

Hate Crimes in Schools

When victims are attacked because of their race, religion, or sexual orientation, the assaults are called hate crimes.

There is no one single cause for these crimes. Some experts on juvenile violence believe that teens attack those who are different because it somehow makes the attackers feel as if they are part of an "in" group. Others believe that teens are simply reacting to messages they get from the adults around them, who include ethnic jokes, racial slurs, and religious put-downs in their daily conversations.

To measure attacks on minorities in schools, Louis Harris, a successful pollster, was hired by the Metropolitan Life Insurance Company to study the problem. His firm has produced in-depth studies on all forms of violence in schools for more than ten years. While conducting the most recent study of hate crimes in schools, his interviewers talked to eighteen hundred high school students in various schools throughout the United States. The interviewers found that confrontations between individuals of different races, faiths, or sexual orientations were commonplace; more than half claimed to have witnessed a racial confrontation, and one fourth said that they had been targets themselves. Only 30 percent of the students said they would make any attempt to stop an incident if they saw one; in fact, most said they would join the attack, claiming that the group being attacked was getting what it deserved.[9]

Teen Victims of Property Crimes

Besides physical assaults, having their property vandalized or stolen is also a risk students take in school. A little over 7 percent of teenage students report at least one property crime each year, many of which involve threats

27

and intimidation. Minority students may find threats or symbols—the Nazi swastika, for example—spray painted on their lockers; others may be forced to hand over their jackets or gold chains under threat of assault.

There are few patterns to the robberies: boys report approximately the same number of robberies as do girls, and students of all races report about the same number of incidents. One trend, though, seems to be the number of times a student has moved. Children from families that have relocated two or more times in the last five years are more likely to be robbed than students whose families have remained in the same area for many years. The second trend is age: ninth-graders reported the most property crimes of any group, more than twice as many incidents as reported by twelfth-graders, who are robbed the least.[10]

Crimes Are Not Reported

Because the number of vandalisms and thefts reported in schools involves only a small fraction of students, it is easy to draw the conclusion that few of these crimes occur. However, the number of thefts committed in schools—as well as the number of other crimes—is much greater than official records show. Most experts believe that only *2 percent* of the students who have been victimized report the crimes.

There are at least three reasons why the vast majority of victims of teen violence in schools fail to contact authorities. First, teens want to try to solve their own problems without adult help. Second, teenagers do not want to be perceived as tattletales, and they fear that other students will see them as just that if they report assaults. Third, students fear retaliation. In one survey, 29 percent of the students interviewed said they would not report a crime because they believed that the assailant would try to punish them.[11] This is a very real concern, for children face their attackers in school every day unless the perpetrators are permanently removed from the buildings. Furthermore, even if the attackers are expelled from school, victims face possible retaliation outside the classroom.

Lasting Effects of Assaults and Property Crimes

Like the witnesses in Mrs. McDavid's room, victims of assaults and thefts—and witnesses to these crimes— become fearful. Students, especially those who have been victimized, avoid wearing certain kinds of clothing, such as the popular brand of shoes or a team jacket currently in demand, that someone might want to steal. They also avoid certain hallways and rest rooms where assaults have occurred, and they steer clear of students who have been in trouble. Safety-minded students also avoid eye contact with fellow students when they walk in the hallways, and they stay close to their friends. To avoid violence on their way to or from school, wary students avoid certain neighborhoods whenever possible. Besides becoming fearful, victims often lose their ability to trust other people, and they become cynical and disrespectful. This, in turn, can lead to confrontations and more violence, which only reinforces the victims' perception that people cannot be trusted.

Some choose to isolate themselves. While refusing to

socialize is harmful at any age, it is especially harmful to teens: they need to find a place among their peers to ease their separation from their families, a necessary step toward independence. Although not all victims in school will become loners, studies show that more than one third do choose to withdraw from classmates.

In addition to lessening the victims' ability to trust others, being assaulted threatens the victims' self-esteem; victims simply do not feel in control of their lives. Again, this is a very threatening feeling to anyone at any age, but it is especially threatening to teens because it occurs at such an important developmental period in their lives. Becoming an independent adult requires a strong sense of self-esteem. Victims may question their self-worth, and if they come up short, they may not seek independence, an emotionally crippling choice.

Although numerous surveys have been conducted about the effect violence has on grades, to date, experts have not been able to show a correlation between violence and poor grades. In the most recent study, only 11 percent of the students questioned believed that their grades were affected by violence in their schools.[12] However, records reveal that the majority of students involved in violent incidents in schools, both victims and aggressors, are those with poorer grades.

Adult Victims in Schools

Not all victims of teen violence in schools are students. More than six thousand teachers are threatened each day, and more than two hundred a day are actually assaulted by students. While few incidents turn deadly,

Deanna McDavid, a popular English teacher, was shot dead in her classroom. "After her family," Ruth Ann Miller, a close friend, said, "[Deanna's] students were the most important people in her life."

as they did in Deanna McDavid's classroom, they are still serious crimes. In one incident, a teacher was threatened by a thirteen-year-old with a loaded gun because the teacher refused to allow the student to pose for a class picture in an offensive T-shirt. Minority teachers have found graffiti and threats scrawled across their classroom doors, and others have received threatening telephone calls. In Ohio, two middle school girls were arrested for plotting to kill their English teacher because the teacher had yelled at them. Before one of their classmates informed the principal, who put an end to the plot, fellow students eagerly placed bets on whether the girls would go through with the crime.

These incidents sometimes intimidate teachers, and the teachers hesitate to discipline students who have a reputation for being violent. This only encourages the feared teens, as well as some others, to use violence to get their way.

Principals are also at risk. They have been harassed for expelling violent students. They have also been killed for doing so, although the reprisal will sometimes come years afterward. A principal in the Midwest was killed several years after he had repeatedly suspended and then expelled a student; the boy's anger grew over the years, turning into a blind rage. Even disciplining students in a minor way can be risky. In a private school in Redlands, California, a principal who was planning to call a thirteen-year-old student's parents regarding a problem in school was shot by the student, who later committed suicide. In short, no one in schools today is safe from becoming a victim of teen violence.

3

Victims in Homes

On February 27, 1995, fifteen-year-old David Freeman and his seventeen-year-old brother, Bryan, allegedly stabbed and beat to death their parents and their eleven-year-old brother, Eric. Eric had been so badly beaten that his face was barely recognizable. The two teens then fled from their Pennsylvania home. They were located and arrested one week later in a small town in Michigan, and they were charged with three counts of murder.

According to the Freemans' neighbors, the two teens had repeatedly quarreled with their parents and on several occasions had even threatened to kill them. For years, the Freeman home had been a scene of bitter arguments about the boys' behavior and their rejection of their parents' religious beliefs. The teens had become so enraged during these arguments that the parents had called in the police to help them control their sons.

When both boys began to take drugs and abuse alcohol, their parents sought counseling for the teens; when that failed, the Freemans admitted their sons for a short time to a rehabilitation center. Besides intensifying the growing conflict between the boys and their parents, the time the teens served at the center made them more violent; there they met members of a hate group, whom David and Bryan decided to imitate and follow. When they returned home, they shaved their heads and had their foreheads tattooed with *Sieg Heil* (a term that means "hail to victory," which the Nazis in Germany used when greeting each other) and *Berserker* (a person who seeks violence). Then the boys began to sneak out of the house at night to drive to hate-group meetings as far away as New Jersey and Michigan.

David and Bryan were also in trouble in school. The teens, both of whom were over six feet tall and weighed more than two hundred pounds each, bullied classmates for lunch money and shouted racial slurs. They often caused a ruckus in class, and when they were disciplined by their principal, Bryan threatened to kill him. Therefore, although everyone was deeply saddened by the teens' brutal and deadly attacks on their parents and brother, no one who knew David and Bryan was greatly surprised by the events that took place that day.

A few days after the Freeman murders and just four miles away, sixteen-year-old Jeffrey Howorth killed his parents, George and Susan Howorth. Their bodies were found beside their home by their older son, Steve.

Mr. Howorth had been shot five times, and Mrs. Howorth's body contained fourteen slugs. Inside the house, Steve found a note written by Jeffrey. This note, according to court records, showed a great deal of ill will toward Jeffrey's parents and the words "I told you I would do it, Steve. You can't say I didn't warn you."[1]

While police searched for Jeffrey, neighbors and friends tried to make sense of what had happened. Unlike the Freeman boys, Jeffrey Howorth was a good student and a member of the varsity swimming team. He also volunteered regularly for projects at his church, where he attended services each Sunday. To most people who knew the family, the murders were a real shock.

Even more shocking than the Freeman or Howorth murders was the Menendez murder trial. The Menendez case, one of the first of its kind, garnered a lot of attention. This case began on August 20, 1989, when police in Beverly Hills, California, found the bloody, mangled bodies of Kitty and José Menendez, whose faces had been nearly blown away by a total of fourteen shotgun blasts fired at the two victims. While the officers searched for clues, rumors of hit men circulated through the community. Who else, people asked one another, could possibly have committed such brutal murders?

Seven months later the police stunned the community by arresting the Menendezes' two sons, nineteen-year-old Eric and twenty-two-year-old Lyle, for their parents' murders. The sons, who were accused of killing the Menendezes in order to inherit $14 million, had aroused suspicion when, instead of grieving over their parents' deaths, they went on a $700,000 shopping spree. Officials' suspicions were confirmed when an informant told police that Lyle and Eric had confessed to killing their parents during a counseling session with their psychologist, a confession the informant had overheard. Eric and Lyle defended their actions by arguing that their parents had abused them. Because the jury could not reach a unanimous verdict in the first trial, Eric and Lyle had to be tried again.

Murdering one's parents is horrifying to the public. Children are supposed to obey, respect, and love their parents. This assures society that children will make future law-abiding citizens. What, the public wonders, would these children do to people who have no claim to their respect and affection? This is a real concern for Americans, because most teens are tried in juvenile court, which does not permit lengthy sentences. As a result, these teens may be back on the street in a very short time.

Patricide

Killing both parents receives a lot of attention, but killing one's father (patricide) or mother (matricide) is not as unique and therefore does not raise the same amount of curiosity. The reason usually given by the accused for killing their fathers, as in the Menendezes' case, is self-defense, and when teens detail the abuse they have endured, it is often difficult to tell who is the real victim.

For example, when a teenage girl returned to her home in Washington, D.C., to pick up some items she had left behind when she moved out, she had a violent encounter with her stepfather. He began to hit her, and she claimed that she had to defend herself. With the help of three teenage friends who were present, she beat the man to death. Because her stepfather had a history of violent behavior, this girl was successfully able to claim self-defense, portraying herself as the real victim.

While some teens said that they killed a family member to protect themselves, others said that they did so to protect someone they love. In one survey in Detroit, where four fathers were killed by their teenage children, all of the defendants claimed that they did so to protect their mothers.

One of the Detroit teen's stories is typical. According to the police report:

> The home was a scene of recurring violence, in which the victim had assaulted his wife and sons, had threatened them with the same weapon [a shotgun] he eventually died by, had even shot at his wife in the past. On the fatal Sunday, the victim was drunk, berating his wife . . . and beating her, when their son acted to terminate the long history of abuse.[2]

Most patricides, about three hundred each year, are committed by boys, and most are excessively violent. It is not unusual for the victims to have multiple wounds, nor is it unusual for the shooting, beating, or stabbing to continue long after the victim is dead.

Matricide

Matricide is relatively rare; only one hundred children, on average, kill their mothers each year. When matricides do occur, teen defendants also claim that they were abused. However, the type of abuse reported usually consists of vicious verbal attacks—humiliating comments made in public and insults and put-downs made to destroy the victim's self-esteem.

One example of a teen arrested for matricide is seventeen-year-old Steven. As a child, Steven had repeatedly been verbally abused by his mother. Eventually, Steven could take no more. At first he tried to escape by running away. When he was caught and brought home, he tried to commit suicide. When his attempt to kill himself failed, he decided to end his misery by killing his mother. He somehow managed to get a gun, and one night while his mother was asleep, he went into her bedroom, put the gun to her head, and fired twice. He was surprised at the amount of blood the shots caused. "When the bullet hit her," he said, "I thought it would be like TV. I thought it would make a little hole. . . . I was frantic and I didn't know what to do. . . . I just stood there, thinking, 'I actually did it.'"[3]

At first Steven tried to cover up the crime. He hid his mother's body in a deserted spot in the country and attempted—unsuccessfully—to clean up all the blood in his mother's bedroom before reporting her disappearance. Eventually, the police saw through Steven's lies, and he was arrested and charged with murder.

It is very difficult to prove verbal abuse and convince a jury that someone is justified in killing because of this abuse. Therefore, Steven's lawyer urged the teen to avoid a jury trial and plead guilty. A judge sentenced Steven to a long prison term.

Sibling Abuse

Few teens who have been abused by their parents actually kill their abusers. Instead, most vent their rage by attacking their parents and other family members. Some experts on juvenile crime who have interviewed violent teens report that one out of three children between the ages of three and seventeen hit their parents each year. Half of these children, according to the interviewers, had been hit by their parents at least once during that time.[4]

Abused children also attack their siblings, especially younger brothers and sisters. Although spouse and child abuse at the hands of parents gets a lot of attention, the greatest abuse in American homes actually occurs between siblings. Interviewers estimate that over 29 million children attack a sibling every year, and more than 2 million have at some time used a gun or knife on a brother or sister. More than half of these attacks were so severe, according to the interviewers, the attacks would have been considered an assault if they had been perpetrated by a stranger on the street. However, in homes where parents are violent, violence between siblings is accepted as normal behavior, and therefore the assaults are not viewed as crimes.[5]

Teens participate in many sibling assaults. In one study, 64 percent of teens aged fifteen to seventeen admitted to hitting, kicking, biting, or slapping a sibling during the past year. The number of violent incidents in the home, just as in school, decreases as children get older, but the level of violence actually escalates: older teens wield knives and guns to settle disputes more often than do younger children.[6]

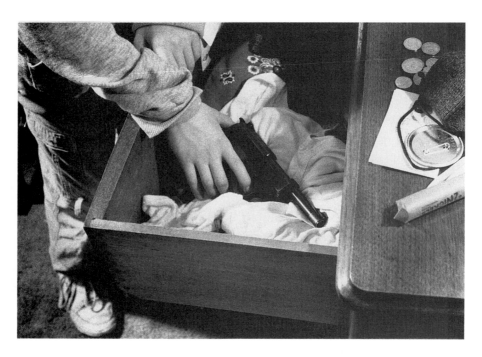

More than two million children have at some time used a knife or gun against their siblings.

Ironically, hitting, kicking, and slapping are regarded as normal behavior by parents, even in homes where parents are not violent toward each other or toward their children. One parent who was questioned about her children said, "They fight all the time. Anything can be a problem . . . but I understand that this is normal. I talk to other people, and their kids are the same way."[7]

Sibling attacks include verbal and sexual abuse, and both, experts believe, are underreported. Unlike fights involving bruises and scratches, repeated name-calling when no one but the victim and tormentor are present can be impossible to prove, and sexual assaults can be embarrassing and painful to report. If victims tell their parents about these assaults, they may not be believed, for it is difficult for mothers and fathers to accept the fact that their children could be guilty of such abuse. If the victim is not believed and the attacker becomes aware of the report, the victim may be at even greater risk of worse abuse in the future.

Although most violent teens make an attempt to explain away or rationalize their behavior, others do not even try, and these senseless attacks are especially shocking. On December 14, 1994, in College Place, Washington, fifteen-year-old Daniel Betournay attacked his fourteen-year-old sister and her best friend when they arrived home from school. According to the police report based on Daniel's confession, the girls at first thought that Daniel was playing some kind of joke on them. But when Daniel bound the girls' hands and feet with duct tape, dragged them into his sister's bedroom, and fastened plastic bags over their heads, they realized that this was not a prank. As the terrified girls began to

41

struggle, trying desperately to remain alive, Daniel calmly walked out of the house. When arrested, Daniel willingly answered all questions about how he killed the girls, but he refused to give any motive for the crimes.

Lasting Effects of Sibling Assaults

Children who have been attacked by siblings and have survived their ordeals continue to suffer long after the assaults stop. Adults who as young people endured degrading comments and name-calling from teenage sisters and brothers report feeling inferior, unloved, and inadequate. One victim who had been insulted repeatedly by her sister said, "I am insecure of my abilities. I lack assertiveness for fear I might verbally be assaulted."[8] Another, a thirty-nine-year-old adult who had been told as a child that she was so fat she was a "cow" said, "I think part of my weight and eating disorder problems are from believing that I was a cow. . . . I have a low self-image and self-worth, and at one time they were so low, I didn't believe anyone would care if I was alive or not. I'm still on antidepressants."[9]

Victims of sibling sexual abuse report feeling worthless and guilty because they believe that they somehow caused the assaults. After the attacks they may be so upset that they try to commit suicide. In a study conducted by Dr. Angela Diaz, chief of adolescent medicine at Mount Sinai Medical Center in New York City, Diaz noted that, among her patients, more than 50 percent of the girls had been sexually assaulted, often at home. These girls experience many effects from their attacks, including depression, dramatic mood swings, chronic tiredness, long-term insomnia, outbursts of anger, and a sudden decline in academic achievement. More than 80 percent of them thought about committing suicide after they were assaulted, and half had attempted to kill themselves, sometimes more than once.[10]

The feelings of guilt do not go away as these victims grow up. Women who were assaulted by their brothers when they were children report long-term effects. One woman told interviewers that she had severe bouts of extreme self-hate long after her brother's attacks had ended. Most also report that they required intensive counseling as adults in order to be able to have healthy relationships with men. These counseling sessions were extremely painful as well as very expensive.

Children of Teenagers

Violent teenagers not only attack parents and siblings, they may also attack their own children. Each year, approximately one million teenage girls become pregnant. According to the National Center for Health Statistics, more than half of these girls will give birth. Some of these babies will be abused by one—and sometimes both—of their teen parents.

Occasionally, the abuse is so severe a child may die. In an incident that occurred in the fall of 1994, a seventeen-year-old father was arrested for beating to death his three-month-old son. This father, who insisted that he was only disciplining the child, had a long criminal record. He had been arrested and tried fifteen times as a juvenile. At the time of his arrest for his son's death, the seventeen-year-old was awaiting trial on two other criminal charges. Because he had so many previous arrests, the judge who was appointed to hear the two charges decided that the teen should be tried as an adult. This way, if he was found guilty, he could be punished more harshly than he could in juvenile court. He was also tried as an adult for his son's death, where he was found guilty of murder.

While not all parents who abuse their children hope that their victims will die, in some cases the child's death is the goal. Such an incident occurred in the autumn of 1994 in a large Midwestern city. There, police received a tip that a newborn baby could be found in a certain garbage can in the city. When police arrived, they found a baby girl who was barely alive. The officers took the infant to a nearby hospital where doctors struggled to save her life.

Two weeks later, police arrested the baby's seventeen-year-old mother and charged her with attempted murder. Her sixteen-year-old girlfriend, who had helped deliver the baby and had encouraged the mother to throw the child away, was also arrested. Shortly after, the girls were tried and found guilty. The mother was given a sentence of five years, and her friend was ordered to serve four; both will be confined to juvenile detention centers. The baby, named Autumn Day, was placed in a foster home after she was released from the hospital.

Outsiders in the Home

A number of violent acts occurring in homes are not caused by family members. On average, more than one hundred ten thousand teens—approximately 10 percent

44

of them girls—break into homes each year, looking for cash and goods they might be able to sell. Sometimes these burglaries turn deadly.

One such incident took place shortly after midnight on April 28, 1991, when six boys and two girls, ages twelve to sixteen, broke into the Simpson household while Mrs. Judith Simpson and her daughter, Amanda, slept. The teens, who took a microwave, left quickly and quietly without disturbing the Simpsons.

The gang was not finished for the night, however. It returned a little while later with a can of gasoline, intent on burning down the Simpson home for reasons that were never stated by the gang. As smoke and flames raced through the house, the teens shouted, "Let 'em burn!"

Neighbors spotted the blaze and called the fire department. By the time the Simpsons were rescued, Amanda and her mother had inhaled a lot of smoke and suffered a number of injuries. Mrs. Simpson recovered from her ordeal, but her daughter did not. Amanda had been a saxophone player, Girl Scout, computer whiz, and volunteer at a local nursing home. She was only twelve years old when she died.[11]

More Arson

Although fire is life-threatening, not all cases of arson result in death. Most fires cause huge property losses, though. Nationwide, more than ten thousand arrests for arson are made each year, and more than half of those arrested are eighteen years old or younger. Children are also involved in one of the largest and most infamous

More than a hundred thousand teens break into homes each year to steal money or goods they can sell.

annual arson incidents, the so-called Devil's Night, which occurs in Detroit, Michigan, each October 31. On Devil's Night, many vacant buildings are set on fire all at once by gangs of teenagers. These fires often spread to homes, creating life-threatening situations. Clearly, a home is not always a haven of safety.

4

Victims Among Friends

The majority of victims of violent teens are other teenagers, and many of these victims have been abused and assaulted—even killed—by their friends. For example, experts on teen violence believe that one out of every four teenage girls may be in an abusive dating relationship, a relationship in which the girl's boyfriend uses psychological or physical means to control and intimidate her. These means may include insults and put-downs as well as slaps, punches, and even rape.

Joyce's case is typical:

> At first, I was flattered my boyfriend Eddie seemed to care so much. Then Eddie began to find faults with little things I did, like the way I carried my books, the way I fixed my hair, why I talked to this person or that person. Then slowly, he started telling me what

to do. At first, I did whatever he asked, hoping to please him. But he was never really pleased. He just criticized something else. Pretty soon, to keep from being scolded, I was asking his advice about everything.[1]

Because she had not been physically assaulted, Joyce refused to believe that she was in an abusive relationship. But when she finally found the courage to differ with Eddie and Eddie slapped her while ranting about all of her "faults," Joyce began to view the relationship very differently. Then she was afraid for her physical well-being, and she discussed the situation with a friend who encouraged her to break up with Eddie. Eddie was enraged when Joyce announced that she would no longer date him. Although he made some frightening threats, she refused to back down and was successful in ending their relationship.

Breaking Up Is Hard to Do

Joyce's decision to stop seeing Eddie was a little easier for her than for most abused girlfriends because she had the support of a close friend. Few victims have such backing. Many girls—and some boys, too—who are in such relationships purposely have been cut off from former friends by their abusers, so that the abusers can better control them. To get and then maintain control, abusers regularly resort to hurling insults and throwing punches at their partners. Eventually, the victims' self-esteem and self-confidence are so weakened by these attacks that they cannot leave their abusers. Most victims believe that

Experts believe that one out of every four girls may be in an abusive dating relationship.

no one will befriend them, and they are afraid to be alone.

In addition, incredible as it may seem, some victims do not see assault as a reason to end a relationship. About 25 percent of the victims in abusive dating relationships have seen or experienced some form of abuse at home, and these victims tend to regard slaps and hits as acceptable treatment.[2] One high school counselor said, "They think [violence] is normal. When we tell them it isn't . . . they're surprised."[3] When informed that violence is not normal, these victims still refuse to break up with their boyfriends "just" because they hit them. In fact, Johna Lovat, a social worker who counsels young women, reported, "Most said it would depend on why he hit her."[4]

Some victims do not end abusive relationships because they think they can change their violent boyfriends or girlfriends. These teens continue to date their abusers, and sometimes they marry them.

The belief that the abuser can be changed is reinforced by the violent partner who, after a round of punching and hitting, usually shows great remorse. Often, the abuser repeatedly promises to change, if only given another chance to do so. During this remorseful period, the abuser often showers the victim with gifts and praise. But another round of insults and attacks almost always follows, for the cycle of violence seldom ends without outside help.

This does not mean that abusers cannot change. Eddie was so upset and taken aback when Joyce refused to date him again that he sought counseling. As a result, he has learned how to control his temper and violent impulses. He, like 75 percent of the boys who assault their girlfriends, was from an abusive home; unlike many of these boys, though, Eddie had the courage and determination to become a different person.

Date Rape

Girls do not have to be in a steady relationship to be attacked by their dates. More than one hundred thousand rapes are reported each year; the greatest number of these are committed by males between the ages of fifteen and twenty-four, and an estimated 60 percent are committed against girls the rapist knows—often on first or second dates.

Victims of rape suffer physical and psychological pain, no matter when, where, or under what circumstances they were attacked. First of all, the victim feels ashamed. This is the result of a commonly held belief that the victim is somehow responsible for the attack. Even victims themselves may accept blame, believing that the way they dressed or something they said caused the attack.

Victims are also hesitant to report a rape because they fear they will not be believed, for it is often only the victim's word against the accused rapist's. If the victim reports the crime and the rapist is arrested and tried, the victim must go through the whole ordeal again—publicly—blow by blow. In the end, the girl may lose the case, her credibility, and her reputation.

In cases of date rape the victim sometimes genuinely cares about the rapist and wishes to protect him. This

SIGNS OF ABUSE

Although both boys and girls can become victims of abusive relationships, the vast majority of victims are girls. How can you tell if a girlfriend is in such a relationship? There are a number of clues to look for, including the following:

- The suspected victim has unexplained bruises.
- The suspected victim sees less and less of her old friends and tends to socialize only with her boyfriend.
- The suspected victim receives a lot of gifts after fights with her boyfriend, which occur often.
- The suspected victim changes hair and clothing styles, often drastically, just to please her boyfriend.
- The suspected victim's boyfriend is very jealous.[5]

makes reporting date rape extremely painful, and some victims simply cannot go through such an ordeal.

These victims, like sexually abused siblings, often suffer long-term effects, especially if they do not seek counseling or avoid it because they are trying to protect the rapist. Most victims suffer from depression, feelings of worthlessness and guilt, as well as extreme moodiness.

Murder Among Friends

Boyfriend-girlfriend abuse and rape are not the only crimes committed by teens against their friends. In fact, one third of all murdered teens were killed by acquaintances and friends—some by very good friends.[6]

Fourteen-year-old Judonne, for example, killed his best friend, Jermaine. Both boys lived in a poverty-stricken area in Washington, D.C., and both had been involved in selling drugs and stealing cars. Judonne's mother, a heavy drug user, gave up her parental rights when Judonne was twelve years old; at the time of the killing, Judonne was living with his grandmother. Jermaine lived with his mother, an unemployed secretary. His father was serving a long prison term for manslaughter and other crimes.

The confrontation between these two friends occurred over a girl. A classmate said, "They both going out with the same girl. . . . [Jermaine] don't know. He find out and get mad. That starts something. . . . Judonne, he just wants to end it."[7]

According to the police report, both boys were armed. When they met in a courtyard, Jermaine told Judonne that he would have to shoot him to keep him away from the girl they both liked. Judonne then fired his gun three times, hitting his friend in the chest. Shortly after Jermaine died, Judonne turned himself in to the police, announcing sadly that he had killed his friend.

Another murder among friends—which made headlines across the United States—took place in Chicago, Illinois. On September 7, 1994, eleven-year-old Yummy Sandifer was gunned down in an underpass on Chicago's South Side by two teenage friends whom he literally trusted with his life.

The startling series of events that led to Sandifer's death began in August 1994. Sandifer, who had a long arrest record and was seeking status in a gang, was supposed to shoot some rival gang members. When Yummy opened fire on the street, he missed his targets and instead shot and killed a young girl, fourteen-year-old Shavon Dean, who was walking a friend home.

The public outrage that followed put intense pressure on the police to find Shavon's killer, and as the police zeroed in on Yummy's gang, gang leaders panicked. They were afraid that Yummy might point a finger at them if he was arrested. They supposedly told two teens in the gang to pretend to help Yummy avoid arrest by driving him out of the city. Shortly after, the teens picked up the boy from his hiding spot, took the eleven-year-old killer to a nearby underpass, and shot him.

While friends and family members mourned the death of Shavon, others gathered to mourn the death of Yummy and to recall the boy's violent life. Born to a teenage mother who was addicted to drugs, Yummy, like his brothers and sisters, was physically abused. He, in turn, abused others, bullying and beating neighborhood children at an early age. Even so, Yummy had friends. One twelve-year-old boy said, "He was my friend, you know? I just cried and cried at school when I heard about what happened. And I'm gonna cry some more today, and I'm gonna cry some more tomorrow, too."[8]

Violence Within Gangs

In part, Yummy's death got as much attention as it did because it was a violent act committed within a gang, and gangs supposedly provide acceptance, support, and protection. But a closer look at gangs and their activities reveals a number of teen victims.

There are at least six hundred gangs in the United States today. Although most street gangs were once found only in large cities such as New York, Chicago, and Los Angeles, gangs have spread throughout the United States and they may be found in 85 percent of all cities with populations of one hundred thousand or more. The number of gang members is estimated to be as high as eighty thousand. Most members are eleven to twenty-one years old.

After being subjected to an initiation rite, which often involves getting viciously beaten to test their loyalty, the newest members are given the most dangerous jobs. As a result, few live long. "If you make it to 19 around here, you are a senior citizen," said one gang member in Chicago. "If you live past that, you're doing real good."[9]

Violence Between Gangs

Many gang members willingly fight other gangs over territory, especially if drug sales are involved. Although some members use drugs, most prefer to sell them for high profits rather than consume them. These profits are then used to buy expensive cars, weapons, and fancy clothes, which, in turn, attract the attention of poverty-stricken youngsters. These children quickly come to think of gangs not only as a source of protection, but as a source of high-paying jobs as well.

The struggle between gangs has resulted in a growing number of victims. According to the U.S. Department of Justice, the number of deaths due to gang killings has increased sixfold from 1980 to the present.

Girls and Gangs

A large number of girls have also joined street gangs. Although no one knows for certain exactly how many teenage girls are members, most sources believe that there are tens of thousands. These girls, like boys, usually join gangs to find support, acceptance, and love. In most cases, they are from homes in which abuse is common and they are just as violent as boys. According to Karen Shonka, a deputy on the Los Angeles Sheriff's Gang Enforcement Team, girls in gangs are "stealing cars, selling drugs, [and] pulling the triggers on drive-by shootings."[10]

Like the boys, girls wanting to join gangs must undergo an initiation. These girls often are either beaten by other gang members for a specific period of time or forced to have sexual relations with boys from a gang that is either associated with the girls' group or in charge of the girls' gang. In one instance, five girls being initiated into a gang were told to have sex with a gang member who claimed that he had AIDS; the girls were so desperate to become members, all agreed to do so. Their plight became known when they went to a clinic to be tested for the AIDS virus—which they did not have.

Although many girls in gangs believe that they are equal to male members, girls are expected to prove their worth by covering for the boys. Margarita Huertas, a gang specialist, said, "The girls do the dirty work. The boys hand them the guns and the drugs when the cops come."[11]

In addition, the girls are often abused by male members. One gang member, Regina, nineteen years old and one of the oldest members of her gang when interviewed, was beaten by her boyfriend because she left a party early. She received a concussion, a split lip, and two black eyes. She was pregnant at the time, and she lost her baby as a result of the beating. "I didn't press charges," she said. "In my 'hood, you don't rat."[12]

Other Victims of Gang Violence

People who are not members of gangs are also affected by gang violence; sometimes entire neighborhoods become victims. After a number of gang shoot-outs took place in one neighborhood, where one incident alone involved a hail of more than forty bullets, even adults reported being afraid to leave their homes. "I don't ever walk up and down the street anymore like I used to," a

Gang-related violence can be found in almost every area of the country. This teen was arrested for shooting a fourteen-year-old rival gang member at a New Year's celebration in a small Midwestern town.

seventy-three-year-old woman said. "I'm afraid to. I just run to the store and back in the house."[13] Another resident wears a hard hat when he leaves his home.

Children who live in violent neighborhoods are not only afraid, they are often traumatized by the violence they see. As a result, some psychiatrists and counselors believe that there may be thousands of young victims suffering from a stress disorder that is similar to what soldiers suffer after combat. Like soldiers, these children complain about recurring nightmares and an inability to concentrate. Also like soldiers, they have seen horrors that remain vivid long afterward. Psychiatrists have reported that children exposed to shooting incidents are often haunted by "the sight, sound and smell of gunfire, the screams or sudden silence of the victim, [and] the splash of blood and tissue on the child's clothes."[14]

More Violent Initiations

Just as street gangs in poor neighborhoods physically abuse their would-be members during initiations, some college fraternities, athletic teams, and bands kidnap, beat, and abuse pledges, mostly young men who want to join the organizations. Called "hazing," this abuse has been common in many universities, including some of the top schools in the nation, for a very long time. The initiations, which are run by members, a number of whom are teens themselves, would be considered assaults if they occurred among strangers, but because they occur among so-called friends, they have simply been considered part of college life. Unfortunately, they have been the cause of many injuries over the years and more than fifty deaths since 1980.

Eileen Stevens's son, Chuck, died of alcohol poisoning during a hazing at a college in upstate New York. Chuck was locked in a car trunk with other pledges in freezing weather. In order to get out of the trunk, the pledges each had to drink a pint of bourbon as well as large quantities of wine. Because Chuck was slow to consume his share and no one could leave the trunk until all the liquor was consumed, one of the pledges forced bourbon and wine down his throat. Chuck died seven hours later, his lungs filled with liquor.

Mrs. Stevens and others have traveled throughout the United States to end hazing. To date, antihazing laws have been passed in thirty-eight states.

This does not mean that hazing has ended, however. In fact, some fraternity advisors estimate that half of all national fraternities defy the law and secretly continue to haze, putting as many as two hundred thousand young men at risk. When sorority and local fraternity pledges are added to this group, the number of young adults facing potential harm is great.[15] Enforcing the law is also difficult; if a fraternity is accused of hazing pledges, a pledge's loyalty to the organization is often so great, he will protect the organization. As journalist Hank Nuwer learned during his investigation of hazing, "Pledges believe so strongly in the fraternity that they are willing to go into court and lie . . . even if they have been physically injured.[16] In short, there will be more victims of this violent action among friends in the future.

Victims in Public Places

The largest number of violent crimes committed by teens occurs in public places. The list of reasons given by violent offenders for attacking their victims is long and varied, and eye-opening.

On May 14, 1993, for instance, fifteen-year-old Charlene Dvork was attacked because she spurned one of her assailants. As Charlene walked along some railroad tracks in Milwaukee, Wisconsin, she was approached by two seventeen-year-old boys, Mark Rea and David Newbury, who attended her school. When Charlene refused to have anything to do with them, they attacked her, knocked her unconscious with a rock, sexually molested her, and beat her with boards before leaving her to die.

Later that day, Newbury returned to the scene of the crime to find out if Charlene was dead yet. She was barely alive when he found her; whether her life might have been saved if he had called an ambulance then is debatable. He deliberately chose not to help her, though, and for the second time that day he walked away from her battered body.

Charlene was finally discovered several hours later and was rushed to a nearby hospital. Although doctors did all they could for her, she died two days later.

Eventually, Rea and Newbury were arrested for the girl's death. The boys were tried as adults, and both were found guilty of first-degree murder.

Newbury, who showed the greatest remorse for the crimes at his trial, had a history of abuse at the hands of his alcoholic parents, and his lawyer asked that this abuse be taken into consideration when the boy was sentenced. Although the judge felt great empathy for David, the judge refused to show any leniency for the horrible crime the boy had committed, in part because David had had an opportunity to help Charlene and had chosen not to do so. Newbury will not be eligible for parole until 2040. Rea, who was the instigator of the attack, will not be eligible until 2070.

Twelve-year-old Dion Green also was attacked because he angered his assailant. Green was sitting on the front porch at his girlfriend's house when several teenagers, whom Dion thought he recognized, appeared on the sidewalk. Friendly and eager to please, Green got up and started to walk toward the teens in order to visit with them. When he called one of the teens by the wrong name, the incorrectly identified teen became irate. He mistakenly believed that Dion was insulting him. The teen then pulled out a pistol and began to beat Dion

David Newbury was sentenced to prison for his participation in the
death of Charlene Dvork. He will not be eligible for parole until 2040.

with the weapon. When Green tried to get away, the teen shot the boy in the back. One of the bullets severely damaged Dion's spine, paralyzing him for life.

Ramon Rios upset his assailants by dressing from head to foot in blue, a color supposedly reserved for members of the notorious Crips gang. When gang members spotted Rios on a Los Angeles bus, they gave him a sign to which he failed to respond. One of the gang members, certain Rios was not a member and therefore ineligible to wear blue, pulled a gun and shot Rios dead in front of fifteen passengers.

Random Targets

Not all victims in public places are people who have angered their assailants. Sometimes these victims were selected at random. For example, on June 24, 1993, near Houston, Texas, at around 11:30 P.M., two teenage girls, Jennifer Ertman and Elizabeth Pena, were trying to get home from a party before their midnight curfew. They took a shortcut through a vacant field and were spotted and assaulted by six teenage boys who had been drinking and fighting at a gang initiation near the edge of the field. The boys raped the girls and then strangled them with shoelaces and belts. When it was apparent that the girls were not dead yet, the assailants took turns jumping on the victims' necks to kill them. The girls' battered bodies were found four days later.

The six teens, who bragged about what they did, were arrested shortly after. One tried to assault reporters as police hauled him away; another boasted that he had finally hit the "big time." The senseless murders and the behavior of the accused enraged the community to the point that they demanded the death penalty.

All six were eventually found guilty of murder, and, as in the Dvork case, no leniency was shown. The youngest, who was seventeen years old, was sentenced to forty years in prison; the others were old enough to be given the death penalty, and they are currently on death row.

One of the most famous cases of a random attack in a public place occurred in April 1989 in New York City's Central Park. Late one night a gang of teens was canvassing the area, looking for victims for a night of what the teens called wilding. They repeatedly insulted a husband and wife who were walking through the park, robbed several young men, and kicked and beat another until he was unconscious. Then they spotted a young woman jogging. They knocked her down and took turns raping her. To muffle her screams they at first gagged her, and when that failed to produce the silence they wanted, they furiously beat her with a metal pipe and pounded her head with rocks, causing multiple skull fractures, until she lost consciousness. Then they pulled out their knives and repeatedly slashed her legs before they finally stopped attacking her.

This young woman, a Wall Street investment banker, lay unconscious for more than three hours before passers-by found her. By then she had lost more than three quarters of her blood and her body temperature was almost twenty degrees below normal. Although her chances of surviving were slim at best, doctors were able to save her life.

Her recovery, although more rapid than anyone

Violent confrontations often occur in public places such as parks.

could have hoped, took a long time. She was not able to return to work until eight months after the attack. Even though doctors did all they could to repair the damage the gang had caused, the jogger still has no sense of smell and, on occasion, she has vision problems and difficulty walking. Despite plastic surgery, the damage to her head and face is still visible and can never be completely erased.

This brutal assault made national headlines, and it horrified and sickened the public. The attackers' behavior after their arrest upset the public even more. The assailants claimed that beating their victim was done just for "fun," and instead of showing remorse after being jailed, they made wisecracks, whistled at a policewoman, and sang a then popular song, "Wild Thing."[1] As in the cases in Wisconsin and Texas, the harshest penalties possible were handed down.

Bystanders

Bystanders can also become victims of angry, violent teens when the intended target is missed. Drive-by shootings often put at risk or include bystanders, such as Shavon Dean, who died when Yummy Sandifer tried to shoot some gang members. If shoot-outs take place in crowded public places, many people are potential victims.

At a mall in Texas, Kevin Bacon, a thirty-seven-year-old electrician, became one of these victims. Bacon had taken his family to the fast-food section of the mall for dinner. While he was carrying a tray to his family's table, two groups of teens got into an argument on the mall's

69

escalator when one group tried to pass another. Bullets began to fly and Bacon was hit. He died while his horrified wife and two little girls watched.

Children have been caught in cross fire as well. In a park in San Fernando, California, a mother and three of her children were injured when two rival gangs decided to shoot it out. The mother and her two sons were hit in the back; their wounds were minor. The mother's ten-year-old daughter was shot in the stomach and head. This girl had to undergo surgery in order to live. In another incident, a little girl was hit in the heart by a stray bullet while she ordered ice cream from a street vendor in Los Angeles.

Robbery Victims

Sometimes victims in public places are attacked because of their possessions. Their assailants want money or a particular jacket, shoes, necklace, or boom box.

Roger Buchholz, a businessman, husband, and father of two children, was targeted by two seventeen-year-olds because they wanted his car. When Buchholz tried to drive away during the attempted robbery, the teens killed him. Supposedly, the assailants decided to steal a car after watching the movie *Menance II Society*. Both were tried as adults. The teen who shot Buchholz will not be eligible for parole until 2038; the other teen was sentenced to prison until 2018.

The boys who shot Buchholz are not the only teens who are in prison for robbery. Approximately one hundred thirty thousand assailants are arrested each year for this crime; among these criminals are thirty-four thousand teens—about 26 percent of all robbers. Boys account for 90 percent of the teens arrested. However, although girls now make up 10 percent of the group arrested for theft, the number of their arrests is increasing each year.

Unlike other crimes, robberies appear to have a pattern. For one thing, people who live in the West and Northeast are at greater risk than people living in the Midwest and the South. Also, people living in cities are more than twice as likely to experience a robbery than people living in suburban areas. The largest number of thefts, 92 percent, take place on the street; only 8 percent occur in the victims' homes.

Hate Crimes

Besides robbery victims, others deliberately targeted in public places are victims of hate crimes. Just as in schools, these crimes are committed against a person because of his or her race, ethnic background, religion, or sexual orientation. How many of these crimes have been committed is difficult to determine because, as with other criminal acts, not all incidents are reported. Also, crimes are usually classified by the crimes themselves—murder, rape, and so on—rather than by motive.

To try to gather numbers, the U.S. Congress passed the Hate Crimes Statistics Act of 1990. This act asks law enforcement agencies across the nation to voluntarily furnish data about hate crimes to federal bureaus so that the problem can be studied more closely. To date, agencies in thirty-two states have supplied at least some information.

The first statistics were analyzed by the Federal Bureau

People who live in large cities are twice as likely to be robbed by violent teens than are citizens in small towns.

of Investigation (FBI) in 1991. That year almost five thousand hate crimes were reported. Of these incidents, a little over 34 percent of the victims were threatened with violence, 33 percent were assaulted, 28 percent had property damaged, and 3 percent were robbed. Less than one percent were murdered or raped.[2]

When questioned about motivation, more than 60 percent of the assailants said that they attacked their victims because of the victim's race. Victims included whites, African Americans, Native Americans, Asians, and even groups consisting of several races—a mix of Asians and Native Americans, for instance. African Americans were attacked more often than any other group. Although the assailants included members of all races, the greatest number of attackers, 65 percent, were white. Researchers also found that 9 percent of hate-crime victims were attacked because of their ethnic background (more than half of these victims were Latinos). Nineteen percent of all hate-crime victims were attacked because of their religious beliefs. Members of the Jewish faith were by and large the most likely to be attacked, making up almost 17 percent of all victims of hate crimes. Although members of other religions, including Catholics, Protestants, and Muslims, were also attacked, altogether they made up less than 2 percent of victims assaulted because of their faith. Ten percent of hate crime victims were attacked because of their sexual preference, whether real or imagined. The vast majority of these victims were selected because they were thought to be homosexuals.[3]

Although the federal government has just begun to keep and analyze records of hate crimes, New York City has kept such records since 1986. These records include information about teens and their involvement in hate crimes. According to New York's records, "between 1986 and 1990, hate crimes jumped 80 percent. And 70 percent of those arrested for hate crimes were under age 19."[4] Daniel Levitas, executive director of the Center for Democratic Renewal in Atlanta, Georgia, which tracks the incidence of racial violence, believes that the rise in hate crimes committed by teens in New York is typical of what is happening all over the country.

Hate Crimes Against African Americans

Teens may not account for all hate crimes, but the incidents in which they have been involved have been deeply upsetting and, in some cases, deadly. One of the most publicized attacks took place on August 23, 1989, in Bensonhurst, a small, predominately white neighborhood in Brooklyn, New York. That fatal day, sixteen-year-old Yusef Hawkins, an African American, and three of his friends went to Bensonhurst to look at a used car, which had been advertised in the paper. Minutes after walking into the neighborhood, the African Americans were spotted by a group of white teens, thirty to forty strong, who chased Hawkins and his friends. At first, the gang was content with chasing Hawkins and the others down the street, shouting racial slurs and threatening to beat them when they caught them. Then one of the pursuing teens tired of the chase. He pulled out his gun and fired at Hawkins, hitting him twice in the chest. Yusef Hawkins died shortly after.

The two teens most responsible for this tragedy

were tried and sentenced the following June. The nineteen-year-old who shot Hawkins was sentenced to thirty-two years to life in prison. The nineteen-year-old who organized the gang and led the chase was sentenced to five to sixteen years.

Not all hate crime assailants have received such stiff sentences. In fact, in another incident in Brooklyn, in the Howard Beach area, the assailants were convicted of "recklessly causing the death of another," a crime that does not carry as long a sentence as murder does.

This incident began late at night on December, 19, 1989, when three African Americans were stranded in Howard Beach after their car broke down. While making plans to find a way home, the men stopped to eat at a restaurant, where they were spotted and then approached by a gang of white teenage thugs. These teens were armed to the teeth with baseball bats, a tire iron, a tree stump, and a lot of hatred. When the three victims saw the angry teens coming toward them, they tried to avoid trouble by running in different directions. One managed to slip away in the darkness. The other two were not as lucky. The second victim was quickly caught and beaten unmercifully. The third, with pursuers nearly breathing down his neck, attempted a desperate escape on the nearby freeway. He climbed over the barricade and successfully crossed three lanes of traffic before being fatally hit by traffic in the fourth lane. He died instantly.

Hate Crimes Against Homosexuals

Gays, too, have been targets of hate crimes. Hate crime assailants have gone into areas where homosexuals are

75

known to socialize, looking for people to harass and beat senseless. According to Matt Foreman, who studies violent incidents aimed at gays:

> Gay-bashing has actually become a fad or sport among certain high school students. In the typical case, two or more young men arm themselves with knives, bottles, hammers, or baseball bats and then target a part of the city in which they suspect that large numbers of gays congregate or reside. The intruders rush in, assault their unsuspecting victim, and rush out again.[5]

Several years ago in Maine, three teenage boys attacked a man they believed to be a homosexual. After beating him, they threw him from a bridge to his death. Then they openly boasted about what they did.

More recently, Marvin McClendon, a seventeen-year-old in Laurel, Mississippi, was arrested for the murder of two homosexual men. At his trial, McClendon claimed self-defense. He insisted that he shot both men to protect himself from being attacked. The district attorney successfully argued that McClendon led the men to a lonely spot on the outskirts of town and shot them only because they were gay. The jury found McClendon guilty of first-degree murder.

Hate Groups

Prejudice and hatred are encouraged by organized hate groups. There are now approximately two hundred fifty such groups in the United States and Canada. Because most of the members of these organizations shave their heads, participants are often referred to as skinheads. Members, who are mostly teens and young adults, believe in white supremacy. They are easy to spot, not only because of their hairstyle but also because of their usual style of dress: heavy boots, leather jackets that are often decorated with Nazi swastikas, and often army fatigues. Skinheads may also utter Nazi slogans or sport Nazi-style tattoos. The Freeman teens (the two teens accused of killing their parents and younger brother in Pennsylvania) were skinheads.

Hate crimes committed by members of such groups include a variety of attacks in public places. In one incident, an eighteen-year-old white supremacist was arrested for attacking an African-American man and his girlfriend as they walked down the street. In other incidents, African-American children have been roughed up on their way to school by white supremacist teens. In California, an eighteen-year-old white youth attending a concert was beaten and stabbed by skinheads who did not like the T-shirt the victim was wearing because it pictured Jimi Hendrix, an African American.

Ironically, members of hate groups can sometimes become victims themselves. Recently, Joe Rowan, a twenty-two-year-old member of a white supremacist group, was shot dead outside a convenience store. Rowan, who had stopped at the store with a number of friends, made racial slurs toward several African-American customers. Tempers flared, and, as Rowan began to walk away, he was shot in the back. A nineteen-year-old African American was arrested for the murder. Whether he will be tried under a hate-crimes law, which allows the judge hearing the case to increase the penalty, is not certain. What is certain is the fact that hate groups are growing; they are actively recruiting teenagers in schools and in homes through a computer network. As the groups grow, the number of victims of hate groups in public places will increase.

6

The Costs of
Teen Violence

Dr. Deborah Prothrow-Stith was a medical intern in the emergency room at a hospital in Boston. One morning, around 3:00 A.M., a nineteen-year-old man arrived at the hospital with a nasty gash just above one of his eyes. As Prothrow-Stith tended the wound, the young man told her what had happened. She recalled later:

> He'd been to a party. . . . He had had quite a lot to drink. A throw-away comment from a guy he barely knew ignited his anger. An argument erupted. Insults were shouted. A crowd of excited on-lookers gathered and began to egg the disputants on. A shove was given, and then a punch was thrown. A knife flashed across the young man's brow. An inch lower and he would have lost his eye. I could see that the young man's anger had not cooled down one bit in the hour since the fight. As I taped a clean bandage over his

stitches, he told me with a swagger, "Don't go to sleep because the guy who did this to me is going to be in here in about an hour."[1]

Unlike this young man, not all victims of teen violence can be treated quickly in emergency rooms and sent on their way. Victims who have had part of their hands or faces or intestines blown away by gunshot wounds or their skulls fractured by blunt objects require lengthy recoveries in a hospital. The Central Park jogger, for example, spent many months in various hospitals recovering from her brutal beating. Sometimes victims shot in the head have so much brain damage that they can no longer function in society; instead, after their wounds have healed, they are taken to institutions, where they will spend the rest of their lives. Some, such as those who have been shot in the back and suffer serious spinal injuries, require lengthy rehabilitation periods after the wounds have healed.

Clearly, victims of teen violence in schools, homes, and public places suffer, but their pain is only one result—one cost, so to speak—of teen violence. There are financial and psychological costs from this violence that greatly lengthen the list of victims.

Medical Costs

Victims of violence run up huge hospital and doctor bills. One study estimates that it costs over fourteen thousand dollars to treat a single gunshot wound in one child—the same sum it takes to send one student to a top university for a year. If the treatment requires a lengthy recovery period in the hospital, the cost could easily rise to one hundred fifty thousand dollars. When all emergency room costs just for gunshot wounds are totaled, the sum is staggering—$4 billion per year. This sum does not include doctor bills, rehabilitation fees, or institutionalization costs. If all injuries for all victims of violence are taken into account, the annual bill is thought to be $60 billion.[2] This shocking sum, which is 10 percent of all medical costs in the United States for a year, is enough to send more than 4 million young adults to college for one year.

The exact portion of medical bills caused by teen violence is difficult to determine; hospitals do not keep records of costs caused by teens separate from those caused by others. Because records indicate that teens have been arrested for more than 20 percent of all violent crimes, they apparently account for much of this cost.

Although criminals in general do not especially target a particular group in our society, many of the victims of violent crimes are poor and unemployed. As a result, most do not have large savings accounts or health insurance. Therefore, unless hospitals are willing to help victims of violence at no cost, taxpayers must pay these bills. Currently, 85 percent of medical costs caused by violence is paid for by the public.[3]

Imprisonment Costs

Rising crime rates have caused an uproar in the United States and the public has repeatedly clamored for more arrests and longer sentences regardless of the age of the criminal. As a result, the number of criminals serving time in prisons—state and federal—has skyrocketed. In

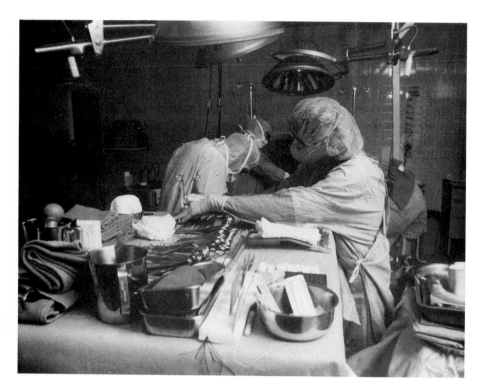
Medical costs have skyrocketed because of injuries caused by violence in the United States.

1980, there were approximately three hundred thirty thousand prisoners in federal institutions; in 1993, there were roughly nine hundred forty-nine thousand, an increase of about 188 percent.[4] At the same time, the American population increased approximately 9 percent.

The increase in arrests has resulted in a big demand for more beds in prisons, almost eighteen hundred more every week. More prisons are being built to accommodate the increase, and the buildings are very expensive to construct. Criminologist Joan Petersilia estimates that "Construction costs typically range between $50,000 and $75,000 *per cell.*"[5] In addition, it costs, on average, at least fourteen thousand dollars to house each inmate for a year. This means that a teen given a long term will cost taxpayers hundreds of thousands of dollars. David Newbury, who murdered Charlene Dvork and will not be eligible for parole until 2040, will cost the public $644,000 for his jailtime—if costs do not go up between now and 2040. His friend Mark Rea, who will not be eligible for parole until 2070, will cost taxpayers $1,064,000.

Because prisons are obviously costly institutions to build and run and do little to change criminals and their behavior—more than 70 percent of teenage criminals are arrested again after serving time—many experts on crime are trying to find less expensive and more effective ways to deal with criminals. They are focusing mostly on teenage criminals. Unless teens have been convicted of the most serious of crimes, they could be sent to a type of boot camp, where it is hoped that strict discipline, physical training, and hard labor might change their behavior.

Others may be sent to juvenile detention facilities

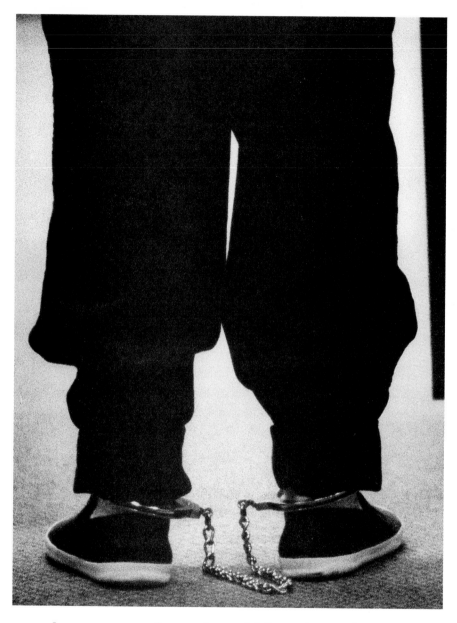

It costs, on average, fourteen thousand dollars each year to house one violent teen.

rather than to prisons to try to keep them away from hardened criminals, who have little to teach teens other than how to become better criminals. However, these centers are often as expensive to run as prisons, and because teens have become so violent, juvenile detention facilities have become almost as violent as prisons. The U.S. Justice Department recently surveyed over nine hundred detention centers. Of the sixty-five thousand juveniles held in these centers, eleven thousand had tried to commit suicide or acts of self-mutilation during that year. At the same time, twenty-four thousand attacks on inmates and eight thousand attacks on staff members were reported.

One of the most recent assaults was an attack on Linda Bratcher, a counselor in a detention facility. She was beaten by two feuding teens when she attempted to stop their fight. Bratcher was seriously injured, suffering a ruptured disk in her back and a blood clot on her kidney that required three surgeries. After two months of rehabilitation for her back, she is still not able to return to work, and doctors are not optimistic about a speedy recovery. If she cannot return to work before her sick leave runs out, Bratcher will be faced with another cost of teen violence when working adults become victims—lost wages.

School Costs

Since so many schools have had problems with teen violence, a number of them have taken steps to protect students and staff members, some of which are rather expensive. Large school systems that have experienced many incidents of violence now hire security officers. New York City, for example, hires more than two thousand officers to patrol schools and surrounding neighborhoods to identify and disarm students who carry weapons. Currently, this costs the city of New York more than $60 million a year in salaries alone.

In addition, school districts are purchasing and installing metal detectors to try to identify students who are carrying weapons so that officials can stop them from entering the school buildings. The least expensive of these detectors, handheld wands that are passed over and around the students and their belongings, cost about one hundred fifteen dollars each. Walk-through detectors sell for around twenty-five hundred dollars each. Because schools must have many exits in case of fire, and because using metal detectors to check students one by one is a slow process, most schools using detectors purchase more than one. When multiple purchases for each school are totaled, the cost is significant. For example, just to install one walk-through device in each of New York's schools would cost more than $2 million.

Many educators believe that the money spent on security systems should be spent on other things. Richard Organisciak, a principal in one of New York City's high schools, said, "I would have used [the money] to buy new books. . . . Instead, we have an expensive security package that doesn't work half the time."[6]

Even so, according to the National School Board Association, 15 percent of the members polled reported that they used detectors in some or all of their schools. Others are currently considering doing the same.

To help schools defray some of the security costs, Congress has proposed and passed several bills to pay for security systems. One of these bills provided $175 million to schools, and Congress has promised to provide more funds in the future.

Further, numerous studies have been commissioned to determine how serious the problems of school safety are as well as what steps should be taken. One of these studies alone cost over $2 million.

Emotional Costs for Survivor-Victims

Many people would limit the number of victims to those actually murdered or attacked. By this definition, the victims in Mrs. McDavid's classroom would be Mrs. McDavid and Mr. Hicks, but all of McDavid's and Hicks's family members and friends were victims also. Each of them experienced intense anger and pain, as well as guilt because they did not somehow prevent the tragedy from taking place. Some experts call them survivor-victims.

The unexpected violent death of a loved one causes extreme anguish, and this psychological pain may last a long time. Kevin Johnson was murdered on the street by a stranger. Four years after his death, his family's emotional scars still had not healed. His brother said:

> It's a terrible thing. I don't think anybody recovers from it. There are too many complications that happen after. . . . My mother has never gotten over it, to this day. My father has become a very nervous man. And my parents are distant from each other now. Somehow they can't comfort each other. We had a very open house—I mean as far as we could always discuss things. . . . But now, my father won't even let us say Kevin's name. . . . Everybody went into themselves.[7]

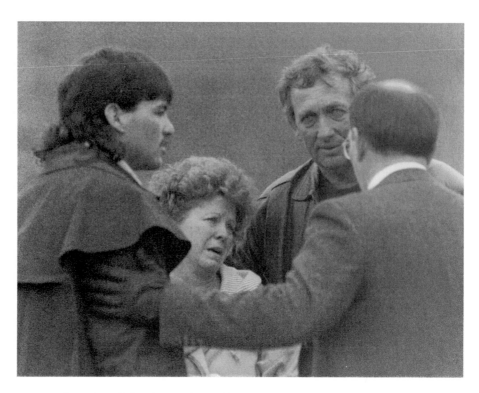

Friends and family members of victims of violent crimes experience great pain. Here an official is shown giving members of Deanna McDavid's family information about her murder.

While everyone seems to understand a parent's grief, a sibling's loss is often treated as if it mattered less. "Everyone told me to be strong for my parents," said eighteen-year-old Lisa after her sister had been murdered. "Everyone told me to put my feelings aside, like my feelings weren't as important as my parents. I never cried until about a year later, when it hit me that my sister Sandy wasn't around."[8]

In recent years, experts have looked more closely at the impact siblings' deaths have on family members. More than one expert believes that the family members who suffer the most are young teenagers. This is due, in part, to the fact that they have the greatest difficulty finding someone with whom they can share their feelings. Friends really cannot understand or appreciate the depth of pain the survivor-victim is experiencing. On the other hand, thirteen-year-olds are often hesitant to turn to family members who can understand the pain and anguish. Dr. Gerald Koocher, a staff psychologist at Children's Hospital in Boston, said, "If I had to pick the family member at greatest emotional risk when a child dies, it would be the adolescent sibling. . . . It's not a time when most kids want to sit down with their folks to talk about feelings."[9]

Often these teens will attempt to make their parents feel better by assuming some of the deceased siblings' characteristics or interests. In this way, they try to keep their brothers or sisters alive. At the same time, these children give up some of their own identities.

In addition to grief, friends and family members of murdered victims also experience overwhelming feelings of guilt. They feel that somehow they are to blame for their loved one's death because they failed to protect him or her. If the survivor-victim actually witnessed the crime and could do little or nothing to protect the victim, he or she may experience feelings of helplessness as well.

Emotional Costs for the Public

Teen violence is painful and frightening, not just to the victims and their families and friends, but to the public in general. Teen crimes are seen as senseless and brutal, and the attitude displayed by violent teens when they are caught greatly upsets the public. These teens are seen as criminals without a conscience, as heartless, impulsive thugs who rejoice in their victims' torment. There are plenty of examples to support this view: the deaths of Charlene Dvork, Elizabeth Pena, and Jennifer Ertman, who were trying to beat a curfew, and the jogger in New York City's Central Park, just to mention a few.

The fear of violence is so great that many people have changed the way they live in hopes of avoiding it. For example, as the number of crimes has risen in Milwaukee, Wisconsin, residents there have changed their lifestyles, and their changes are not so different from people in other large cities. Of the four hundred citizens interviewed, 54 percent of the women and 28 percent of the men said they were afraid to walk alone at night. Because of this fear, 29 percent of the women and 15 percent of the men now stay home after dark, and about

When parents bury a child, they also bury all the hopes and dreams they had for the child. Almost three hundred teenagers are murdered each year by their peers.

half of these admitted to losing sleep at night because of their fear of becoming victims.[10] Others have invested in expensive security systems and locks for their homes, taken self-defense classes, and purchased guns. In short, violence has made victims of many people, even those who have not been robbed, raped, or assaulted.

7

Fighting Back

Reading mystery books and watching whodunits on television are popular pastimes in America. Besides enjoying the stories, mystery enthusiasts love to try to figure out who the guilty party is long before the book or program ends. In order to make identifying the murderers difficult, mystery writers create many suspects who might want the victims dead. Typically, victims are pictured as conniving, mean-spirited critters who have hurt many people over the years. Often when the murderers are finally revealed, they try to explain away their actions, blaming the victims' deaths on the victims themselves because of some cruel act they committed.

Likewise, the notion that real-life victims do something to cause their victimization is widely accepted, even among victims. Rape and sexual assault victims are among the most willing targets to assume responsibility for their assaults, wondering whether or not something they said or the way they dressed caused their assailants to strike. These victims believe that if they can find a cause for their attacks—a cause that they can control—they can avoid attacks in the future. Often they fail to blame the person responsible—the rapist—believing that the attack was a crime of passion, not an attack meant solely to hurt and humiliate.

Victims also blame themselves because of something they did not do, believing that if they had taken proper precautions, they could have stopped any would-be assailant. The following responses from two victims are typical. One said, "I think my lack of caution had a lot to do with the fact that my apartment was burglarized, and I take responsibility for that."[1] Another victim, who was assaulted while she waited for a bus in a neighborhood with a high crime rate, also took the blame for her attack. She felt responsible because she did not take a taxi. After being attacked, she said, "I took a chance and I got caught. I feel responsible in that I did something I knew I shouldn't have done."[2]

While some victims of teen violence are like the evil characters in mystery books—brutal, abusive parents, for example—experts on crime believe that the vast majority of victims of teen violence are what are known as innocent victims. They did not pose any threat to their assailants, nor did they in any way harm them. In fact, many victims of teen violence had never even seen their attackers before the crimes were committed. The two girls murdered in a vacant field in Texas, Yusuf Hawkins who went to Bensonhurst only to buy a car, and most victims of hate crimes, for example, did not know their murderers. These victims simply happened upon violent people.

The belief that every person should somehow be able to avoid being attacked makes victims feel ashamed when they are assaulted. Embarrassment often prevents them from admitting that an attack took place and is one of the reasons only half of the crimes occurring in the United States are reported. Shame also prevents victims from reaching out to others for support during a very difficult time. One victim said, "I just hate to think of myself as a victim. It's like when I lost my job . . . it was so embarrassing to have to tell people that I had lost my job. And when this [robbery] happened, I felt the same way. It was like a guilty secret."[3]

On the other hand, if victims do decide to talk about the assault, they still may not find the support they need. Many listeners become embarrassed and simply back away, especially if the victim becomes emotional. Americans admire and respect winners and strong people. Victims who have clearly lost something and are in need of help are often looked down upon. They are thought of as losers and weaklings, incapable of protecting themselves.

Ironically, it is the criminal who usually receives a lot of attention when a crime is committed. He or she may even become a popular figure. One of the most famous violent characters in American history was Billy the Kid, who began his criminal career in his late teens and eventually killed twenty-one men before he was gunned down himself. Dozens of books have been written about him over the years, but to date not one has been written about the men he shot.

People are genuinely curious about people who are unusual, and criminals are unusual. Therefore, teen killers who are especially brutal or very young catch the public's attention. For example, Yummy Sandifer, the eleven-year-old gang member shot in Chicago, was the subject of many news reports on television as well as every news magazine. He was pictured even on some magazine covers. The public not only wants to know more about such people, it also wants to be reassured that these criminals are so unusual that it is doubtful there are more like them.

Perception of Victims Is Changing

The traditional view of victims—they are responsible for what happens to them and weak to boot—slowly began to change during the 1970s and 1980s. Although a number of groups of people who had been victimized began to speak out, two particular groups had the most significant effect on the victims' rights movement: battered wives and victims of drunk drivers.

For generations, women who were abused by their husbands generally kept their abuse a secret. It was believed by many that husbands had the right to discipline their wives by whatever means they chose to use. This belief was based upon ancient customs that made the husband the head of the household and upon laws that made it legal for a husband to beat his wife in order to make her obey. This attitude prevailed well into the 1960s. In fact, in 1960, when a woman in California

96

who left her husband because he beat her tried to sue him for damages, the court refused to hear her case. The judge regarded the attacks not as criminal but as a private matter about which the court could not interfere. Also, it was commonly believed that any wife who was beaten had done something to deserve such treatment.

But in the 1970s, as women began an all-out drive for equal rights, some battered wives began to speak out and fight back. They demanded to have their cases heard in court, and although few won in the beginning, the women's stories made a deep impression on the public. When a judge in Colorado sentenced a man who had killed his wife to two years' probation, women's groups and their supporters were outraged. Public pressure was great, forcing the judge—who had said that the husband's actions were justified because his wife had left him—to reconsider his sentence and to watch his tongue more closely in the future. As more and more stories came to light, the public began to change its attitude toward battered wives, and it began to hold responsible the men who did the beating, rather than the women who were beaten.

In 1980, Candy Lightner's teenage daughter was killed by a hit-and-run drunk driver. At that time, men and women who drove while intoxicated were seldom held responsible for their actions, because people under the influence of alcohol allegedly do not know what they are doing. Dead or maimed victims were simply said to have been in the wrong place at the wrong time, much like what was said about the jogger in Central Park. When Candy Lightner learned that the man who killed her daughter—a man who had four prior arrests for driving while drunk—would probably never be punished, she vowed to change the way the system worked.

Shortly after, Lightner founded a remarkably successful organization called Mothers Against Drunk Driving (MADD). This national organization dedicated itself to getting justice for all victims of drunk drivers by stating that drunk drivers make a conscious decision to drink and drive, and therefore they should be held responsible for the harm they cause. MADD won over many people and lawmakers, and as a result intoxicated drivers now face stiff penalties—hefty fines and jail time—for driving while drunk.

As battered wives and victims of drunk drivers gained public support, innocent victims of violent crimes also cried out for justice. They were sick and tired of being ashamed, fed up with being made to feel that they were responsible for their attacks, and unwilling to assume the costs of their victimization.

Victim Compensation Programs

The hue and cry of victims of violent crimes drew the attention and support of state legislators throughout the United States who then drafted, debated, and passed compensation bills in one state after another. By 1992, all states had passed laws that offered financial help to these victims.

Although compensation programs vary from state to state, they have a number of similarities. First, any innocent victim of a violent crime may apply for financial aid in the state where the crime took place. Second, the victim must have reported the crime to the police, usually

Candy Lightner started Mothers Against Drunk Driving (MADD) after her teenage daughter was killed by an intoxicated driver. Each year, approximately ten thousand teens are arrested for driving under the influence of alcohol.

within seventy-two hours after the assault. Third, the victim must agree to cooperate with police in solving and prosecuting the crime. However, the criminal need not be arrested in order for the victim to qualify for aid.

Victims or their survivors may apply for funds to pay a variety of bills. All states will now accept requests for funds for medical bills, lost wages, funeral costs, and the costs of counseling. Some states will even pay counseling costs for witnesses of violent crimes. The victim compensation program is a program of last resort, though, and victims may not apply if health insurance, disability insurance, or other kinds of insurance will pay the victims' or the survivors' expenses. Most states have a maximum amount allowed; California currently has a limit of fifty thousand dollars, while Georgia will provide only one thousand.

The money used to fund these programs comes from three sources. Local courts fine citizens for a variety of offenses, driving too fast or driving while drunk, for example. A portion of these funds is used to finance each state's victim compensation program. The federal government also provides funds to each state with money it raises by fining people and organizations who have broken federal laws. The federal courts usually collect about $150 million per year, which they parcel out to the states. The rest of the money comes from state taxpayers.

Other Sources of Compensation

Victims of violent crimes may also sue their assailants, but because few teenagers have a great deal of money or property, this approach is not often used by victims of

Who Is Eligible?

An innocent victim who suffers injury from a crime.

A dependent or legal representative of an innocent victim who has been killed as a result of a crime.

A person who is injured while aiding a crime victim or helping a police officer.

A person who suffers a reaction from the death of a family or household member.

Persons who are injured in automobile accidents caused by drunk drivers.

What Compensation May Be Paid?

Up to $40,000 for any one injury or death including:

- Medical, hospital, surgical, pharmacy, and mental health counseling expenses.
- Lost wages.
- Loss of support to a dependent of a crime victim who is killed.
- Reasonable replacement costs of clothing or bedding held as evidence by the police, prosecutor, or crime lab, up to $300.
- Reasonable replacement value for property held as evidence and made unusable by crime lab testing, up to $200.
- Reasonable and necessary costs for securing and cleaning a crime scene, up to $1,000.
- Cost of homemaker services.

An additional $2,000 may be paid for reasonable funeral expenses.

No property loss or damage is covered other than described above.

Up to $500 is available for immediate emergency expenses if the victim is employed but cannot work due to injuries from the crime.

The State of Wisconsin pays only those out of pocket expenses that are not paid or payable by a private or group insurance plan, public funds, or any other source, including the offender. If you receive monies from the offender or a third party through restitution or any civil action, you must repay the state for any monies paid out on your behalf.

What Are The Requirements?

The victim's conduct must not have caused or contributed to the crime that led to the injury or death.

The victim must not have committed a crime that led to the injury or death.

The victim must cooperate with law enforcement officials in their investigation and prosecution of the crime.

The applicant must cooperate with the Wisconsin Department of Justice in supplying information for the claim.

If the victim was injured in a car accident caused by a drunk driver, he/she must have been:

- a pedestrian or passenger in the other car.
- a child passenger in the offender's car.
- unaware that the driver was under the influence of alcohol or an illegal drug.
- legally sober, with a blood alcohol concentration below .1%.

What Must I Do To Be Eligible?

The crime must have been reported to a law enforcement agency within 5 days of the crime.

The applicant must file a claim within 1 year of the date of the crime. This may be waived in certain circumstances.

The program cannot make any payment on a claim until the victim is current with court ordered child support or maintenance payments.

This flier contains a summary of the victims' compensation program in one state, Wisconsin.

teen violence. However, because courts will allow victims to put a claim on any earnings of their assailants, victims may be able to obtain money sometime in the future. Also, some states have financial restitution programs for teenagers, in which teens are given jobs for a set wage and a portion of those wages is given to the victims.

Help in Court

Sometimes victims need help to face their assailants in court, and many states now provide advocates to assist them. The advocates accompany victims when they testify and refer them to various resources that can help them before and after the trial. This assistance is especially valuable for children who fear facing a room full of spectators, lawyers, newspaper reporters, and a judge all by themselves. It also makes it more likely that children will press charges.

Other Sources of Help

Victims of violent crimes often need counseling to deal with the many emotions—anger, guilt, helplessness, depression—that victimization causes. Private counseling is available to both children and adults; counseling can be very expensive, but victim compensation plans may cover some or all of the costs.

Children may also receive help at no cost in their schools. If a large number of students has been affected by a violent crime—such as the shootings in Deanna McDavid's room—counselors who have been trained specifically to deal with violent events and their aftermath may be brought to the schools where the tragedies occurred to meet with students. After McDavid's death,

DJ-CVC-1, Rev. 7/90

CRIME VICTIM COMPENSATION APPLICATION

Return to: **WISCONSIN DEPARTMENT OF JUSTICE**
Crime Victim Compensation Program
Post Office Box 7951
Madison, Wisconsin 53707-7951

CVC File:
No._____

INSTRUCTIONS

Before completing this application, please read these instructior ~rv carefully.

1. Please print or type clearly.

2. If sufficient space is not provided on this form, use additional sheets as necessary.

3. If you need any help in completing the application, call:

   In Milwaukee   (414) 227-3987
   In Madison   (608) 266-6470
   Wisconsin Toll-free   1-800-446-6564

4. An application must be filed within 1 year of the date of the crime. If it is being filed after that time period, please call this office to see if tha' requirement may be waived.

5. The ' ~ he signed by the victim
   or tʰ '^he victim is under
   18 '~ death of a
   viʳ ʰᵥ the
   s
   ,

6.

WHEN CRIME STRIKES

injured victims can get help

I. VICTIM INFORMATION

Victim's name _____

Street address _____

City/State/Zip _____

Social security number _____

Spouse's name _____

emale

/_____

IF PERSON COMPLETING THE ...NG:

Wisconsin Department Of Justice
Crime Victim Compensation Program
James E. Doyle, Attorney General

Name _____

Address _____

)_____

Victims of violent crimes in many states must complete application forms before they are eligible for compensation.

for example, a special counselor was brought in, and he held daily sessions for over a month with students who witnessed the shootings.

Private organizations will also help victims of teen violence. Victims of sibling abuse at home or abuse at the hands of a boyfriend can receive help at shelters for battered women, many of which are listed in telephone books. Rape victims can receive help at rape crisis centers. Again, most of these centers are listed in telephone books.

Numerous support groups can help victims of teen violence as well. Often members of these groups have been victimized themselves, and they truly understand what the victim is going through. Lists of such organizations are usually available through local social services offices.

The number of organizations established just to help victims is constantly growing, and as the image of victims continues to change, more victims will be willing to reach out and receive the help these groups can give. In fact, being a victim has become a status symbol among some young people. Two teenage boys in a Midwestern town recently shot themselves so that they could claim they had been hit in a drive-by shooting and, they hoped, get a lot of attention from classmates, especially the girls. It did not take the police long to figure out that the boys' story was not true, and within hours after they had their stomach wounds treated, both boys were in a lot of trouble as well as pain.

Stopping the Violence

Potential victims cannot stop every criminal act simply by locking doors and avoiding dangerous neighborhoods.

Therefore, instead of making violent teens look around a little harder for victims, numerous programs have been started in a serious attempt to stop teen violence. States have passed stricter gun laws designed to keep guns out of the hands of children. Legislators have also reviewed juvenile justice codes, and many are considering making it possible to try juveniles as adults at a younger age and making prison sentences longer. Whether these actions will act as deterrents and result in a decrease in the number of crimes committed by teenagers remains to be seen.

Executing juveniles has also been suggested as a deterrent, and it is currently a hotly debated topic. Victor Streib, an expert on juvenile violence, said, "We're at a crossroads. There's near hysteria now about juvenile crime, so I'm not surprised at communities' grabbing at the death penalty as a solution. We're not really sure what to do at this point."[4]

Various groups are also pressuring the media to limit the amount of violence shown on television. Less than fifteen years ago, most comedians included skits about drunks in their routines, skits that were often considered hilarious. Today, thanks to MADD, being drunk is no longer thought of as funny. Advocates for children's television programs hope to bring about as dramatic an attitude change toward violence: Violence is neither glamorous nor acceptable. Period.

Peer Mediation

A number of programs aimed at preventing teen violence have been developed by schools. These include counseling and installing hot lines for students to call.

Scott Pennington is only one of a number of teens tried for crimes for which prosecutors have asked for the death penalty. He was sentenced to life.

One of the most promising programs, though, is peer mediation, which is now used in more than five thousand school systems. Peer mediation programs encourage teens to settle their differences peacefully and without adult interference. Teen volunteers in the participating schools are taught how to spot trouble and how to intervene. When an incident occurs, the volunteers isolate the upset students, listen to both sides, and try to get the students to discuss their differences and arrive at a peaceful settlement. It may take all day to get an agreement, but once it is reached, the feuding parties put the agreement in writing and sign it. In one school where the program was just started, forty agreements had been signed, and only one of these had been broken. Mediation programs work in large part because all sides can save face, and no one's dignity or self-esteem is assaulted.

The Future

Even though steps are being taken to curb teen violence, the problem is so widespread that it is not likely to disappear in the very near future. Therefore, the number of victims of teen violence will increase. Although dramatic changes in attitude toward victims has occurred over the last ten years and compensation programs have been developed, more help may be required. Experts wonder if the compensation programs are adequate. They question whether the programs should be standardized, that is, made the same in all states, and they wonder if these victims—especially children—need other forms of help.

REDUCING VIOLENCE IN SCHOOLS

Recently, twenty-five hundred students were asked to evaluate programs that their school had started to try to stop violence. The students' opinions are listed below.

PROGRAM	VERY SUCCESSFUL	SOMEWHAT SUCCESSFUL	NOT SUCCESSFUL
Class meetings	22 percent	60 percent	18 percent
Speakers about crime and violence	29 percent	54 percent	17 percent
Hot line for students to call	27 percent	38 percent	35 percent
Counseling for students and their families	29 percent	52 percent	19 percent
Classes on how to solve problems without resorting to violence	24 percent	51 percent	25 percent
Monitors in the halls	27 percent	49 percent	24 percent
Security guards in school	36 percent	46 percent	18 percent
Metal detectors	22 percent	30 percent	48 percent
Random checks of belongings and lockers	23 percent	47 percent	30 percent
Suspended or expelled violent students	43 percent	41 percent	16 percent[5]

Now that you know more about the issue of teen violence and its victims, what do you think should be done? What steps should be taken to curb teen violence in schools? In the home? In public places? Should victims be given more help by school officials? By their peers? By the government? By private organizations? What can each of us do to help the victims of teen violence? What can each of us do to help stop it?

Help for Victims

The following national organizations provide information about victims' rights, as well as information about local support groups.

National Association of Crime Victim Compensation Boards
P.O. Box 16003
Alexandria, VA 22302
(703) 370-2996

National Organization for Victim Assistance
1757 Park Road, N.W.
Washington, DC 20010-2101
(202) 232-NOVA
(800) 879-NOVA

National Victim Center
309 West 7th Street, Suite 705
Fort Worth, TX 76102
(703) 276-2880
(800) FYI-CALL

Clearinghouse on Family Violence Information
P.O. Box 1182
Washington, DC 20013
(703) 385-7565

Center for Democratic Renewal (hate crimes)
P.O. Box 50469
Atlanta, GA 30302
(404) 221-0025

Crime Victims Research and Treatment Center
Medical University—University of South Carolina
171 Ashley Avenue
Charleston, SC 29425
(803) 792-2945

Children of Murdered Parents
P.O. Box 9317
Whittier, CA 90608
(310) 699-8427

Parents of Murdered Children
100 East 8th Street
Cincinnati, OH 45202
(513) 721-5683

Chapter Notes

Chapter 1

1. U.S. Department of Justice.

2. Adam Walinsky, "The Crisis of Public Order," *The Atlantic Monthly* (July 1995), p. 49.

3. U.S. Department of Justice.

4. Phil Sude, "A Tide of Teen Violence," *Scholastic Update* (April 5, 1991), p. 4.

5. Michael D. Biskup and Charles P. Cozic, eds., *Youth Violence* (San Diego: Greenhaven Press, 1992), p. 70.

6. Renardo Barden, *Juvenile Violence* (New York: Marshall Cavendish, 1994), p. 37.

7. James Earl Hardy, "Killing for Clothes," *Scholastic Update* (April 5, 1991), p. 7.

8. "Fighting Crime Before It Happens," *U.S. News & World Report* (March 17, 1986), p. 28.

Chapter 2

1. Michael D. Biskup and Charles P. Cozic, eds., *Youth Violence* (San Diego: Greenhaven Press, 1992), p. 28.

2. Thomas Tock, "Violence Goes to School," *U.S. & World Report* (November 8, 1993), p. 32.

3. Ibid. p. 30.

4. Jerry Buckley, "The Tragedy in Room 108," *U.S. News and World Report* (November 8, 1993), p. 46.

5. Louis Harris and Associates, Inc.

6. Robert Leitman, *The Metropolitan Life Survey of the American Teacher 1994. Violence in America's Public Schools: The Family Perspective* (New York: Louis Harris and Associates, Inc., 1995), p. 51.

7. Lisa D. Bastian and Bruce M. Taylor, *School Crime: A National Crime Victimization Survey Report* (Washington, D.C.: U.S. Government Printing Office, 1991), p. 2.

8. Biskup and Cozic, pp. 115–117.

9. Jack Levin and Jack McDevitt, *Hate Crimes* (New York: Plenum Press, 1993), p. 117.

10. Bastian and Taylor, p. 1.

11. Leitman, p. 118.

12. Ibid. p. 61.

Chapter 3

1. "Church-going Teen Sought in Murders," *The Oshkosh Northwestern* (March 4, 1995), p. A2.

2. Martin Daly and Margo Wilson, *Homicide* (New York: Aldine De Gruyter, 1988), p. 98.

3. Paul A. Mones, *When a Child Kills: Abused Children Who Kill Their Parents* (New York: Pocket Books, 1991), p. 179.

4. Murray A. Straus, Richard J. Gelles, and Suzanne K. Steinmetz, *Behind Closed Doors: Violence in the American Family* (Garden City, N.Y.: Anchor Press, 1980), p. 120.

5. Ibid. pp. 81–82, 117.

6. Ibid. pp. 86, 90.

7. Ibid. p. 79.

8. Vernon R. Wiehe, *Sibling Abuse: Hidden Physical, Emotional, and Sexual Trauma* (Lexington, Mass.: D.C. Heath and Company, 1990), p. 110.

9. Ibid. p. 111.

10. Leslie Laurence, "Time to Level with Teen-age Girls," *The Oshkosh Northwestern* (January 10, 1995), p. D2.

11. Michael D. Biskup and Charles P. Cozic, eds., *Youth Violence* (San Diego: Greenhaven Press, 1992), p. 122.

Chapter 4

1. Renardo Barden, *Juvenile Violence* (New York: Marshall Cavendish, 1994), pp. 67–68.

2. Valerie Chow Bush, "Battered Girlfriends," *Scholastic Update* (April 5, 1991), p. 9.

3. Sandy Mickelson, "Reports of Abuse Rising Among City Teen-agers," *The Oshkosh Northwestern* (November 7, 1994), p. A1.

4. Ibid.

5. Kathy Connolly, Children's Advocate, Regional Domestic Abuse Center, Oshkosh, Wisconsin.

6. Deborah Prothrow-Stith, *Deadly Consequences* (New York: HarperCollins, 1991), p. 21.

7. Michael D. Biskup and Charles P. Cozic, eds., *Youth Violence* (San Diego: Greenhaven Press, 1992), p. 21.

8. Nancy R. Gibbs, "Murder in Miniature," *Time* (September 19, 1994), p. 59.

9. Ibid. p. 58.

10. Gini Sikes, "Girls in the 'Hood," *Scholastic Update* (February 11, 1994), p. 21.

11. "Equal Rights in Violence," *The Oshkosh Northwestern* (September 18, 1994), p. F2.

12. Sikes, p. 21.

13. Jim Stingl and Mary Carole McCauley, "Gangs' Game of One-upmanship Has Deadly Outcome," *The Milwaukee Journal* (September 18, 1994), p. B4.

14. Biskup and Cozic, p. 26.

15. Hank Nuwer, *Broken Pledges: The Deadly Rite of Hazing* (Marietta, Ga.: Longstreet Press, Inc., 1990), p. 240.

16. Ibid. p. 214.

Chapter 5

1. Michael D. Biskup and Charles P. Cozic, eds., *Youth Violence* (San Diego: Greenhaven Press, 1992), Preface.

2. *Information Please Almanac 1994* (Boston and New York: Houghton Mifflin Co., 1994), p. 853.

3. Ibid.

4. Katie Monagle, "When Teens Hate," *Scholastic Update* (April 5, 1991), p. 7.

5. Jack Levin and Jack McDevitt, *Hate Crimes* (New York: Plenum Press, 1993), p. 71.

Chapter 6

1. Deborah Prothrow-Stith, *Deadly Consequences* (New York: HarperCollins, 1991), p. 2.

2. Ibid. p. 20.

3. Ibid.

4. U.S. Department of Justice, *Prisoners in 1993* (Washington, D.C.: U.S. Government Printing Office, 1995), p. 1.

5. *What Are the Alternatives to Prisons?* (San Diego: Greenhaven Press, 1991), p. 211.

6. Karen N. Peart, "Lessons in Survival," *Scholastic Update* (February 11, 1994), p. 17.

7. Morton Bard and Dawn Sangrey, *The Crime Victim's Book* (New York: Brunner/Mazel, 1986), pp. 13–14.

8. Elizabeth Richter, "How the Death of a Child Hurts Brothers and Sisters: 'Did I Really Love My Brother?'" *U.S. News & World Report* (August 4, 1986), p. 60.

9. Ibid.

10. Jeff Browne, "Fear Drives Us into Hiding," *Milwaukee Journal* (October 25, 1994), p. A1.

Chapter 7

1. Morton Bard and Dawn Sangrey, *The Crime Victim's Book* (New York: Brunner/Mazel, 1986), p. 56.

2. Ibid.

3. Ibid. p. 76.

4. "Cities Grapple with Dealing Death to Juveniles," *The Oshkosh Northwestern* (October 25, 1994), p. A1.

5. Louis Harris and Associates, Inc.

Bibliography

Bard, Morton, and Dawn Sangrey. *The Crime Victim's Book*. New York: Brunner/Mazel Publishers, 1986.

Barden, Renardo. *Juvenile Violence*. New York: Marshall Cavendish, 1993.

Bastian, Liza D., and Bruce M. Taylor. *School Crime: A National Crime Victimization Survey Report*. Washington, D.C.: U.S. Government Printing Office, 1991.

Biskup, Michael D., and Charles P. Cozic, eds. *Youth Violence*. San Diego: Greenhaven Press, 1992.

Brown, Charles G. *First Get Mad, Then Get Justice*. Secaucus, N.J.: Carol Publishing Group, 1993.

Browne, Jeff. "Fear Drives Us into Hiding." *Milwaukee Journal* (October 25, 1994), A1.

Buckley, Jerry. "The Tragedy in Room 108." *U.S. News & World Report* (November 8, 1993), 41–46.

Bush, Valerie Chow. "Battered Girlfriends." *Scholastic Update* (April 5, 1991), 9.

"Church-going Teen Sought in Murders." *Oshkosh Northwestern* (March 4, 1995), A2.

"Cities Grapple with Dealing Death to Juveniles." *Oshkosh Northwestern* (October 25, 1994), A1.

Daly, Martin, and Margo Wilson. *Homicide.* Hawthorne, N.Y.: Aldine De Gruyter, 1988.

Drevitch, Gary. "River of Blood, River of Tears." *Scholastic Update* (February 11, 1994), 4–7.

"Equal Rights in Violence." *The Oshkosh Northwestern* (September 18, 1994), F2.

"Fighting Crime Before It Happens." *U.S. News & World Report* (March 17, 1986), 28.

Gelman, David. "The Violence in Our Heads." *Newsweek* (August 2, 1993), 48.

Gibbs, Nancy R. "Murder in Miniature." *Time* (September 19, 1994), 54–59.

Hardy, James Earl. "Killing for Clothes." *Scholastic Update* (April 5, 1991), 6–7.

Heide, Kathleen M. *Why Kids Kill Parents.* Columbus, Ohio: Ohio State University Press, 1992.

Information Please Almanac 1994. Boston and New York: Houghton Mifflin Co., 1994.

Lacayo, Richard. "When Kids Go Bad." *Time* (September 19, 1994), 60–63.

Laurence, Leslie. "Time to Level with Teen-age Girls." *Oshkosh Northwestern* (January 10, 1995), D2.

Leitman, Robert. *The Metropolitan Life Survey of the American Teacher 1994. Violence in America's Public Schools: The Family Perspective.* New York: Louis Harris and Associates, Inc., 1995.

Levin, Jack, and Jack McDevitt. *Hate Crimes.* New York: Plenum Press, 1993.

McBride, Geralyn. "Shooting Victim Linked to White Supremacist Group." *Milwaukee Journal* (October 2, 1994), B1.

Mickelson, Sandy. "Reports of Abuse Rising Among City Teen-agers." *Oshkosh Northwestern* (November 7, 1994), A1.

Monagle, Katie. "When Teens Hate." *Scholastic Update* (April 5, 1991), 7–8.

Mones, Paul A. *When a Child Kills: Abused Children Who Kill Their Parents.* New York: Pocket Books, 1991.

Netzer, Mary Jo. "Impressive? Boys Shoot Themselves in Stomachs to Be Cool." *Oshkosh Northwestern* (December 9, 1993), A1.

"Number of Condemned now 5 in Deaths of Teens." *Oshkosh Northwestern* (September 26, 1994), B8.

Nuwer, Hank. *Broken Pledges: The Deadly Rite of Hazing.* Marietta, Ga.: Longstreet Press, Inc., 1990.

Peart, Karen N. "Lessons in Survival." *Scholastic Update* (February 11, 1994), 17.

Prothrow-Stith, Deborah. *Deadly Consequences.* New York: HarperCollins, 1991.

Richter, Elizabeth. "How the Death of a Child Hurts Brothers and Sisters: 'Did I Really Love My Brother?'" *U.S. News & World Report* (August 4, 1986), 60.

121

Rummler, Gary C. "Violence and Kids: An Unnerving Cycle." *Milwaukee Journal* (January 16, 1994), G1, G4.

Sikes, Gini. "Girls in the 'Hood." *Scholastic Update* (February 11, 1994), 20–21.

Stingl, Jim. "Dvork Case: Young Killer Weeps as He Gets Life Term." *Milwaukee Journal* (December 18, 1993), B1, B4.

———, and Mary Carole McCauley. "Gangs' Game of One-upmanship Has Deadly Outcome." *Milwaukee Journal* (September 18, 1994), B4.

Straus, Murray A., Richard J. Gelles, and Suzanne K. Steinmetz. *Behind Closed Doors: Violence in the American Family.* Garden City, N.Y.: Anchor Press, 1980.

Sude, Phil. "A Tide of Teen Violence." *Scholastic Update* (April 5, 1991), 4.

Thompson, Dick. "The Exploding Costs of Gunfire." *Time* (October 11, 1993), 59.

Tock, Thomas. "Violence Goes to School." *U.S. News & World Report* (November 8, 1993), 30.

Walinsky, Adam. "The Crisis of Public Order." *The Atlantic Monthly* (July, 1995), 39–54.

What Are the Alternatives to Prisons? San Diego: Greenhaven Press, 1991.

Wiehe, Vernon R. *Sibling Abuse.* Lexington, Mass.: Lexington Books, 1990.

Zawitz, Marianne W., Patsy A. Klaus, Ronet Bachman, Lisa D. Bastian, Marshall M. DeBerry, Jr., Michael R. Rand, and Bruce M. Taylor. *Highlights from 20 Years of Surveying Crime Victims: The National Crime Victimization Survey, 1973–92.* Washington D.C.: U.S. Government Printing Office, 1993.

Further Reading

Barden, Renardo. *Gangs*. Vero Beach, Fla.: Rourke, 1990.

Barden's book discusses the issues that lead to the formation of gangs, including poverty, racism, and drugs.

Barden, Renardo. *Juvenile Violence*. New York: Marshall Cavendish, 1994.

This book was written for young people who are afraid of crime. The text explores many kinds of violence—sex abuse, date rape, gang violence—and describes actions readers should take to protect themselves from becoming victims.

Blue, Rose. *Working Together Against Hate Groups*. New York: Rosen Publishing Group, 1994.

Blue discusses hate crimes against minorities and how people working together can prevent them.

Landau, Elaine. *Child Abuse: An American Epidemic*. Englewood Cliffs, N.J.: Julian Messner, 1989.

This book explores the many causes of child abuse and what can be done to help abused children. Of special interest is a list of agencies and organizations that can help these victims, regardless of who abused them, whether parents or siblings.

Also, because teen violence is a topic of great interest, many newspapers and magazines regularly feature stories and summaries of the latest surveys. For newspaper articles, scan issues from large cities, especially papers from New York, Chicago, Detroit, and Washington,

125

D.C. Most libraries subscribe to at least one paper from one of these cities. Major incidents, such as the shootings in Mrs. McDavid's classroom, often make major news magazines, such as *Time* and *U.S. News & World Report.* Use the Reader's Guide to Periodical Literature in your library to locate these articles, many of which can be found under the headings "school violence" and "victims of crime."

Index